Arnold's Ancient Axioms

Typography
for
Publications Editors

EDMUND C. ARNOLD

The Ragan Report Press
Chicago, 1978

To Matthew, Stephen
& Allison — may they
have ink on their fingers.

86 85 84   7 6 5

Printed in the United States of America
Lawrence Ragan Communications, Inc.
407 S. Dearborn St.
Chicago, IL 60605

ISBN 0-931368-02-2

Table of Contents

1

Typographic Procedures

The Ancient Axioms of Typography.

That orotund phrase suggests that typography is an exotic art to be practiced only by those who have been initiated into the mysteries of its dark magic.

Not so. Typography is merely the administration of common sense to the visual, non-verbal elements of communication.

There is no legislation, no divine revelation about typography. But there are some guidelines—sometimes called "Arnold's Ancient Axioms"—that can be useful to the harried editor. The very first of these is:

★ ANCIENT AXIOM NUMBER ONE: Take all axioms with a grain of salt.

For the Axioms are only guidelines. If you follow them, you won't go wrong—at least not far wrong. But to set off sky rockets and trumpet flourishes, you must add that dash of genius that often requires the bending of the guidelines.

To bend the guidelines effectively, though, editors must know them well. More important, they must know the underlying principles of The Axioms. These principles have been determined by sound research of reading mechanism and reader habit, bolstered by sound practical experience and interpreted by sound thinking.

All axioms are based on the reaction of the reader. The "Gutenberg diagram" gives the ground rules for reader action and editor preparation for same.

The eye enters a page, or any subdivision thereof, in the top-left corner. This is the "primary optical area", the "POA". From there it progresses on a general "reading diagonal" to the lower right corner, the "terminal area", or "TA", which is the end of the page and the point from where the reader normally proceeds to the next page.

To lure the eye off this diagonal, especially into the two "fallow corners", "optical magnets" are placed throughout the area.

The reading diagonal is also called "reading gravity", an apt name. For the pull on the reader's eye is as strong and constant as the pull of physical gravity on our bodies. And, even as we don't like to climb stairs, ladders or steep hills, so the reading eye resists attempts to make it go against its gravity. That means upwards, to the left or anywhere in the quadrant.

There is an important exception to resistance against backward movements. When the eye finishes a line of type, it will without protest swing back to read the next line. It does travel against gravity then.

But in that return, the eye wants to come back to a constant starting point, the beginning of the first line, the "axis of orientation", "A/O".

If type is set with a ragged-left margin, the eye still returns to the A/O but must then look for the start of the next line. This is a mental irritation. Worse, it breaks the clean, even, pendulum-like swing of the eye which produces most efficient reading.

★ANCIENT AXIOM NUMBER TWO: Type should be used to communicate, not ornament.

The editor's basic job is always and only to communicate. It is not to create beautiful designs as on shower curtains or kitchen linoleum. Any temptation to use typographic elements "chust for purty" must be sternly stifled.

★ANCIENT AXIOM NUMBER THREE: Typography must be functional.

Every element on a page must contribute to communication. We test each element separately by posing a couple of questions:

"Does this element do a useful, necessary job?"

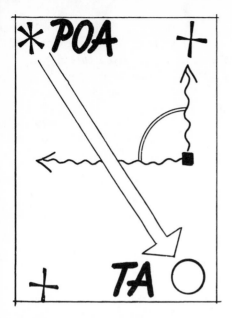

GUTENBERG DIAGRAM charts basic reading eye movement from POA to TA. Crosses indicate fallow corners and arc of wavy lines shows "backward" movement that reading eye resists.

If the answer is yes, we ask: "Can we do this necessary job more quickly, more easily, more efficiently?"

Now we examine the multitudinous options open to us. Often we find that the way we are doing it now is the best way . . . at least for now. So we stick with the present element and its use; but we have the pleasant assurance that we are doing this by decision and not by habit or the legacy of a departed editor.

If, however, the answer to the first question is no, or even just a dubious silence, our immediate reaction is: "Throw it out!" For: ★ANCIENT AXIOM NUMBER FOUR: Non-functional typographic elements are almost always mal-functional. (From here on in, Ancient Axioms will be identified by the star only, for numbers indicate priorities or importance. And the following Axioms are all of equal importance.)

An element that doesn't do a good job usually does a bad one. If it doesn't attract a reader, it distracts him. If it doesn't clarify communications, it puts static into the channel.

Before we throw out a non-functional element, we check our decision by the final question: "What is the worst thing that could happen if I've guessed wrong on this?"

The worst thing that can ever happen is to lose readership. Would that happen in *this* instance if we removed *this* element? Usually the answer to that is, "If the presence of this element doesn't build readership, its elimination won't destroy it either." And then, reassured, we do throw out the non-working element.

Typical non-functional elements that have been eliminated by editors over the past few years are "column rules", horizontal "cutoff rules", second and third "decks" of headlines, "gim-cracks" and "30-dashes".

Useless ornamentation has been stripped away but all ornamentation has not been eliminated. For humans like—indeed they need—ornamentation.

★Ornamentation must be functional.

Ornamentation comes in many forms—editorial color, mood photos, connotative line art, illumination of letters, etc., etc. Whatever its form, it must attract readers, guide the eye through the entire layout, give non-verbal reinforcement to the written message and create a mood in the reader that is receptive to the message. At least one of these functions must be served; the more that any ornamentation can fulfill, the better its use.

★Don't let functionalism make your pages sterile and dull.

The unappealing concrete boxes that pose as contemporary architecture demonstrate what happens when all graciousness is unthinkingly removed from our everyday lives and jobs.

The editor has two tools for communicating: Content and form. Content, the words that articulate a verbal message, is the more important of the two. Humans think in words so they must communicate in words. Non-verbal elements must be translated into verbal in order to achieve clear, precise transfer of information.

But form is also important. Primary forms are the alphabet, the absolute necessity, of course, of written or printed communications. So those 52 characters, the a-through-z's, and the A-through-Z's, are the editor's main tools, irreplaceable ones.

This suggests that the editor have at least a "smattering of ignorance" about the terms that the typesetter and the printer use as they produce our publications.

4

Printers measure the height of type and type lines in "points". One inch equals 72 points. Twelve points equal one "pica", the increment used to measure horizontal line lengths.

An 8-point typeface—in theory, at least—measures 8 points, 8/72 or 1/9 inch, from the very top of the tallest character to the bottom of the tails of letters. That tallest character may be a capital letter or a small letter such as *t* or *h*. The tails or descenders are usually all the same length, as those in *p, y* and *g*.

All letters align on the bottom on a "baseline", be they capitals—also called "upper case"—or small letters, "lower case". "Primary letters" align at the top of a "meanline"; these are characters such as *a, c, m, x,* etc. The projections themselves, as well as the whole letters, are also called "ascenders".

Those that extend below the baseline—*g, j, q,* etc.—are called "descenders" as are the tails themselves.

There is a tiny bit of space between the tails of one line and the ascenders or caps of the one below. That's why an 8-point face won't quite measure 8 points from top to bottom.

Extra space between lines is called "ledding". It's spelled that way, phonetically, in many professional books including this one. But Mr. Webster spells it "leading" in case you are a lexicographical purist.

Because there are literally thousands of different faces an editor can use, a system of classification has been adopted.

There are six type races: Roman, Text, Monotonal, Square Serifs, Written and Ornamented. They are—all except Text—divided into "ethnic groups".

"Roman" has thick and thin strokes, curves that swell, then

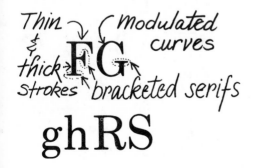

OLD STYLE ROMAN

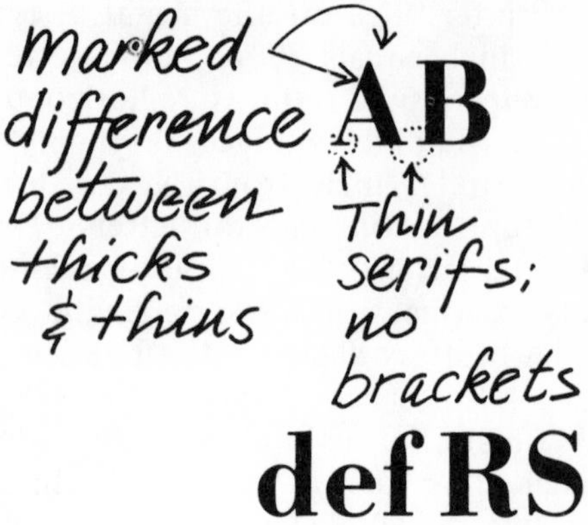

marked difference between thicks & thins

Thin serifs; no brackets

AB

MODERN ROMAN

def RS

diminish, and "serifs", tiny finishing strokes at the end of main strokes. "Modern Roman"—one ethnic group—has marked difference between thicks and thins and its serifs are thin and straight.

"Oldstyle Roman"—the other ethnic—has less difference in weight of strokes. Its serifs are . thicker and are "bracketed", joined to the main stroke by curves. The circular "bowls" of Oldstyle letterforms seem to tilt to the left.

Romans are the workhorses of communications.

"Text" or "Black Letter" is commonly—but incorrectly—known as "Old English". (This is like calling all automobiles Chevrolets.) It is made of thick and thin strokes, angular and compressed. It's rarely used; usually only to head obituary col-

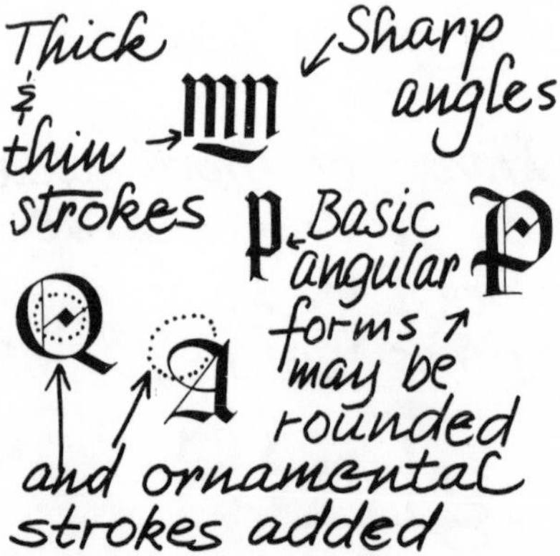

TEXT OR BLACK LETTER.
Examples are of Goudy Text, family of unusual beauty.

Thick & thin strokes

Sharp angles

mn

Basic angular forms may be rounded and ornamental strokes added

All strokes of same thickness

AB
O

no serifs

Bowls based on circle

efg

umns or to say "Merry Christmas".

The "Monotonals", as the name indicates, are made up of strokes of equal weight. They have no serifs. There are two ethnic groups, "Sans Serifs" and "Gothic". Most of the differences are rather technical. The typical editor need only to know that—very generally speaking—Sans Serifs letterforms are based on circles and Gothics on ovals. So the Sans are usually more graceful.

"Square Serifs" are Monotonals to which serifs are added. But not the tiny finishing strokes of the Roman race, heck no! The Squares have serifs at least as heavy as the main strokes. In that case they're in the "Egyptian" ethnic group. If the serifs are heavier than the main strokes, the ethnic is "American".

Egyptian Squares make good headlines; American Squares have such a strong flavor of the Wild West and rodeos that they're generally used only as connotation of that era of our history.

"Written" letterforms are self-explanatory. If the letters are joined, the ethnic group is "Script"; if they're not joined—no

GOTHIC ETHNIC GROUP

Bowls are oval

QR

monotonal
no serifs

Ungraceful curves

Bowls "pinch"

def

as they meet stem

If serifs are heavier than main strokes, the face is an American ↓ Square

Monotonal, **efg**
letterforms → **EF**
Serifs ———
*same weight
as main strokes*

abcdefghijklm

ABCDEFGHIJ

matter how slight the separation between letters—they're "Cursive". There are a great number of Written forms that vary so greatly that they have many uses. Usually they are accents to more formal letterforms.

The "Ornamented" ("ed", not "al") race has three ethnic groups. The first two start out as members of the other races. Then, if something is added to the outside of the letter, it becomes a "Shadowed" face. If something is done to the face of the letter, it becomes a "Shaded" ethnic. If the letterform is drastically changed—letters made of human forms, or rope or flowers, for instance—the ethnic is "Novelty". These, too, are used rarely and

abcdefghijk

abcdefghijklm

*When letters ↑
are joined, they're
Script*

*when not joined,
they're Cursive ↓*

abcdefghijklm

abcdee fghijkl

WRITTEN RACE

8

ORNAMENTED RACE has three ethnic groups.

Adding something to the outside of a face makes a shadowed form.

Doing anything to the face itself makes it shaded.

KL XYZ AB ab

Markedly unusual letter-forms are novelties

then only to give flavor to a page.

New technology makes it possible to offer new typefaces at low cost. Editors are tempted to use eccentric faces just because they are striking and, above all, new. All too often legibility is sacrificed to novelty and the reader is poorly served. The design of letters is just one—but a major one—of the precepts that apply to all typography:

★ KISS!

That means, "Keep it simple, stupid!" Even without the last word—or maybe even better without it—this Ancient Axiom is one that's so important it ought to be—and probably will be—repeated several times in this book.

Type ethnic groups subdivide into "families". Like humans, such type groups have family names. Like ours, these may be the names of the father (or designer)—Goudy, Cooper, Garamond. Or they may suggest a regional origin—Scotch, Karnak, El Dorado. Or they may be just names—Tempo, Stymie, Century.

Like the family look that makes you look like your siblings, the basic letter design remains constant. But variations occur that make you look different from your relatives. With type, variations may be made on angle, width and weight.

Light | ABCDEFGHIJKLMNOPQRST
| abcdefghijklmnopqrstuvwxyz

Medium | ABCDEFGHIJKLMNOPQRST
| abcdefghijklmnopqrstuvwxy

Demi-Bold | ABCDEFGHIJKLMNOPQ
| abcdefghijklmnopqrstuvw

Bold | **ABCDEFGHIJKLMNO**
| **abcdefghijklmnopqrst**

Black | **ABCDEFGHIJKLMN**
| **abcdefghijklmnopq**

FIVE SERIES, plus their Oblique forms (not shown), make up Airport family of type. Weight named "Medium" is normal and often is referred to simply by family name.

If a typeface slants to the right, it's called "Italic". (Technically only slanted Romans are called Italic; all other races' tilted forms are "Oblique". But common usage is to apply "Italic" to all races except Text; it never slants.)

A face retaining its height but widened is called "Extended"; one which is narrowed but keeps the same height is called "Condensed".

Changing the weight of the strokes in a letterform may darken or lighten the character. The most common weighting creates boldface. Even heavier strokes result in "Demibold", "Black", "Heavy" or similarly-termed varieties. Some faces are made with finer strokes in their "Light" or "Book" variety.

Condensed **ABCDEF**   **M**

Normal **ABCDEF**   **M**

Extended **ABCDEF**   **M**

WIDTH VARIATION of normal Cheltenham Bold creates Condensed and Extended.

ANGLE OF LETTERFORM is changed to create Italic version of Roman face and Oblique of other races, Sans Serifs here. Slanting to left creates "Backslant", unpleasant form which is used most infrequently.

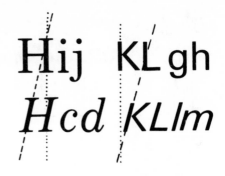

Any such variation is a "series". The series is identified by the family name plus one or more adjectives that indicate variations on the family look. "Caledonia Italic" is a typical series name; it means that the regular Caledonia (the family name) face has been slanted to the right.

Two or even three variations may be made upon a type design, each becoming a series. "Cheltenham Bold Condensed" is a typical series name indicating variations in both weight and width.

When only the family name is used, it means that this is the "Regular" or "Normal" design. We rarely use those adjectives, though. So a name like "Optima" refers not only to that family but also to the basic series thereof, "Optima Regular".

The final type classification is the "font". This is a series in a specific size. Thus the font name always has a size designation like "12-point Palatino Italic".

The editor first uses this terminology when "specifying type". That term is so awkward on the tongue that we simply say "spec type"—with a hard *c*. Speccing is giving the instructions for the typesetter to do the job properly. The editor must give the name of the type, the "duplex", point size, ledding and line length or "measure".

The duplex is the face you want when you underscore a word. Usually it's boldface in newspaper usage, Italics in magazines. But it must be clearly specified. So typically we'd spec type as:

Bodoni with Italic, 9-on-10 - - - - - 18 picas

Here the type size is 9-point. We add an extra point of ledding, space between lines, and that makes the total space from one line to another—or the height of one line, if you prefer that termino-

To do THIS ⬇ ⬇   *use this mark ... and you get this* ⬇

SPELL OUT	by(Wis.)regulations	by Wisconsin regulations
ABBREVIATE	in Detroit,(Michigan)	in Detroit, Mich.
CLOSE UP	for down‿style headlines	for downstyle headlines
INSERT SPACE	(state sales⧧tax ((space between‿words	state sales tax space between words
INSERT	research departmᵉnt	research department
CORRECT ERROR	the reseaᵣch	the research department
LOWERCASE	shipping /department	shipping department
CAPITALIZE	Salt Lake city, Utah	Salt Lake City, Utah
TRANSPOSE	(price of unl␣e␣ded gas ((to (slowly/walk) toward	price of unleaded gas to walk slowly toward
DELETE	to a ~~complete~~ stop	to a stop
DELETE AND CLOSE UP	Letters to the eddⁱtor	letters to the editor

COPYREADING MARKS are used by editor to change manuscript. Note similarity to proofreader's marks but that correction is made at point of error, not in margin.

LET IT STAND	Leave copy ~~just~~ *STET* as it was in original form	Leave copy just as it was in original form
CONNECT MATTER	this copy will connect ~~without any blank space~~ to these words	this copy will connect to these words
CONNECT MATTER	sentence ends. But no new paragraph is desired here.	sentence ends. But no new paragraph is desired here.
PARAGRAPH	This mark calls attention of typesetter to start new paragraph. When we need a new paragraph, this mark is used. Then the next sentence is indented in the customary fashion.	When we need a new paragraph, this mark is used. Then the next sentence is indented in the customary fashion.
NO PARAGRAPH	sentence ends. *no ¶* What is now a separate graf runs in with the previous one.	sentence ends. What is now a separate graf runs in with the previous one.
RUN IN	Twenty-year pins went to: Emma Kinsley, Correen Fairwelt, Timothy Hayes John Sutherland and Oswald Innester *Run in*	Twenty-year pins went to: Emma Kinsley, Correen Fairwelt, Timothy Hayes, John Sutherland and Oswald Innester.
FOLLOW UNUSUAL COPY	*FOLO COPY* The United Steaks of America or United Steaks (CQ) of America	The United Steaks of America United Steaks of America

13

EMPHASIZE PUNCTUATION	Circle periods to keep them from
	being overlooked⊙ And use inverted
	⌄carets⌄ to call attention to
	quotation marks⊙
ITALICIZE	The typesetter <u>will</u> now set "will" in Italics.
BOLDFACE	The typesetter <u>will</u> now set "will" in boldface.
MORE COPY	This story continues on another page. *(MORE)*
END MARK	This is the end of this story. ⧧
	or
	This is the end of this story. —30—

logy—10 points. Hence, 9-point type on a 10-point space. (The instructions may also be written "9/10".)

Eighteen picas is the measure, the length of the line.

Headlines need only be designated by face and point size as the copy shows each line separately. Or a numerical code (which is discussed in Chapter 3) is used. Thus:

"24-pt. Helvetica Medium", or

"2-24" (which means 2 columns wide, 24-point of the regular headletter). Italics is shown with an X: "2-24X". Or one number higher in point size is used. Thus "2-25" would be "2 columns, 24-point Italic".

★Regular procedures make more efficient and easier editing.

While editing is an art, it is also a skill. Good tools enhance any skill and improve any product. After the editor has polished a piece of copy to make it accurate, interesting, taut and color-ful—as well as consistent in style—editorial procedure becomes one of preparing copy for the printer.

★Do all editing on the manuscript.

This costs no more than the editor's time and savvy. Editing changes done on proofs—called "author's alterations" or "AAs"—are extra costs charged at rates even higher than the original typesetting costs.

14

First in USA
Solar Energy Will Heat Michigan Research Center

Solar heat will be used in the addition to the Research and Development Department. A new method invented in Switzerland will be used for the first time in the United States. "This new innovation will return our investment in only 5 years, says Mr. Henry P. Marchfield, vice-president for R&D. "Other methods would take much longer to pay for themselves."

But Chairman of the Board R. M. Danville said that conserving energy is the major consideration, not only dollar savings.

A major consideration in this region is storing heat against days when the sun isn't shining. Plainfield the average 68 days without sunshine annually.

The swiss method heats an unusual mixture of silicon tetraoxide with H_2O_2 peroxide and a trace of the rare metal berylium. This sluggish fluid will hold 4 times as much heat as the same volume of water.

Against a slanting roof facing south west, will be twelve by eighteen heat collecting panels that (more)

EDITED COPY shows slug in top left. Headline is marked with 2-digit code. Typesetter is informed that copy continues onto another page by "(more)".

★Identify all copy.

Each piece of copy should carry a "slugline" that identifies its contents, the author's name and the issue for which it's designated. Thus:

ANNUAL REPORT
Smith
March 2

If copy runs more than one page, this is noted by the signal (MORE) at the bottom of each page. At the end of the story, we use a "30-mark"—either "30", "xxx", "end" or whatever seems appropriate. This enables the typesetter to spot any missing sheets of copy.

★Maintain a copy log.

The "copy log" is a record of all material that the editor has prepared and sent to the typesetter or platemaker. It is invaluable in keeping track of stories yet to come, heads that must be written after the body story has been sent out, the size of pictures sent to the platemaker, etc. The editor uses data from the log when, later, pages are dummied. ("HTK"—"head to come"—is written on all unheaded stories.)

To keep the log, our first job is converting measurements of typewritten copy into measurements of type. For this we need a "mathematical factor". Although this sounds foreboding, it's really not a numerical ogre at all.

All typewritten copy should be typed at a constant line-length. (As always, typewriter lines will vary in length. But if you keep within three characters over or under your standard, they'll even off.) But. . .

★Don't hyphenate words to maintain even typewriter line lengths.

Use a hyphen in typewritten copy only when you want a hyphen to appear in type. The term may be used as "typeset" or as "type-set". If the editor, in order to maintain an even line-length in a manuscript, were to end a line with ". . .type-" it would have the same effect as ending it with ". . .Valen-". The words, in type, would come out "typeset" and "Valentines" with no hyphens showing.

So, if a word is far, far too long for the typewritten line, x it

16

out and put the whole word on the next line. And make sure that when you want a hyphen to occur in the type, you typewrite that word within a line of the manuscript, never at the end or broken over from one line to the next.

When you have established a length for your typewritten line, note the number of characters in it.

Then note the number of characters in an average line of set type. Determine this by counting 20 lines and finding the average. Count spaces between words as one character. Don't use lines with paragraph indents or "widows", lines not completely filled.

Now divide the set-type number into the typewritten number. The result will be your "line factor".

Suppose your typewriter is set for 72-character lines and one line of set type averages 40 characters. Dividing 72 by 40 gives us 1.8 as the factor.

Now we need only to count our typewritten lines, multiply by our factor, and we know the number of typeset lines that we'll have.

We often measure the "editorial hole", space available for all matter in a publication except advertising, in "column-inches". This is an area as wide as one standard column and one inch deep.

We know how many lines of type are in a column-inch. If we don't, we simply measure off five inches of type, count the lines and divide by five. If the result is a weird fraction, count the lines in a 10-inch column. If you get a fraction, carry it only to one decimal place.

Now divide this number into the number of lines of type that our factoring gave us in the previous procedure and we know how many column-inches of type we'll have once our typewritten copy gets typeset.

(You've already noticed the awkward phraseology required to distinguish between typewritten and typeset material. It sure isn't elegant diction, but it is necessary to keep constant distinction between the two kinds of material. Misunderstanding of these terms creates horrendous confusion and, often, needless expenditure of time, money and nervous tension.)

An even better unit for measuring is the "BL", short for "body line". This is the height of a line of body type plus its extra

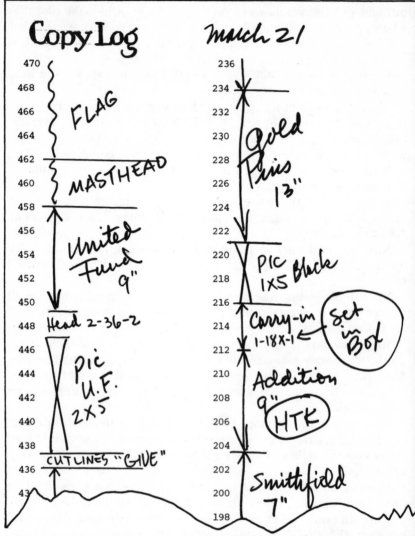

Copy Log   *march 21*

470
468
466 FLAG
464
462 ——— MASTHEAD
460
458 —X—
456
454 United
452 Fund 9"
450 ↓
448 Head 2-36-2
446
444 Pic
442 U.F.
440 2X5
438
436 CUTLINES "_GIVE_" ↑
43

236
234 —X—
232
230 Gold
228 Prins
226 13"
224
222 ↓
220 —X—
218 PIC 1X5 Black
216 —X—
214 Carry-in (Set in Box)
212 1-18X-1 ←
210 Addition
208 9"
206 (HTK)
204 —X—
202
200 Smithfield 7"
198

COPY LOG fragment shows constants indicated by wavy line; news copy by straight line and arrows; pictures by X's. Other pertinent information is circled. "HTK" means "head to come later".

18

ledding. As our first typewriter-to-typesetting conversion gives us the number of BLs, and we know how many BLs there are in the editorial hole, we need only convert all other typographic elements such as heads, photos and other art into the same unit of measurement.

No matter how wide the copy will ultimately be set, reduce it to 1-column BLs.

Suppose there are 8 BLs per vertical inch. You have a picture 2 columns wide by 5 inches deep. Multiply 5 inches by 8 BLs, that's 40, and then by 2 because there are 40 BLs in depth and the pic is 2 columns wide.

Now, to actually keep a copy log:

Determine how many BLs are available in your whole publication. Then make a list, in descending order, from that number of BLs. This may be in increments of 2 to 5 lines.

Suppose this is 3,072. Subtract all "constants"—nameplate, masthead, etc. That brings you, let's say, to 2,920 BLs for fresh

X-HEIGHT is shown by small x's; it's height of primary letters. Taller X's indicate height of corresponding capital letters and, usually, of ascenders. X-heights of faces of same point-size may vary greatly but sizes shown here are average for cold type. Long ascenders or descenders reduce x-height by using greater portion of available height and area designated by point size.

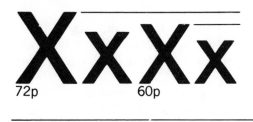

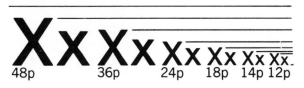

material. Draw a red mark on your copy log at that point.

Now you handle a story of 32 BLs; subtract that number and underline 2,888. The head you write for this story is 1½ inches deep, so subtract 12 BLs. Now you have 2,876.

Do this with every piece of copy, verbal or art, that you prepare. You will always know just how many inches are left for you to fill.

At the end of your cycle, you may note that you're running long on copy. With a major story or two still out, you have only a column of type. Immediately you can start contingency planning. Which stories can I hold till next issue? What picture can be made a column narrower? Are there paragraphs or sections within stories that must run that can be excised?

Conversely, when you seem to be running short, you can run feature material from your reserves.

As you mark off a story on the log, you also write its slugline and any information that will come in useful later when you start dummying up. Type set 1½- or 2-column measure is an example.

The next editorial step is "proofreading". This is examining galley proofs to purge them of typographical errors.

★Meticulous proofreading is the mark of an excellent editor.

The first proofs the editor gets are "galley proofs", long strips of paper with, usually, 1-column setting. The best way to proofread galleys is by the "book method".

First check the galleys to make sure the proper typeface and ledding have been used and that the measure, the line-length, is correct.

Then skim through to see that the type makes sense, that it hasn't been garbled or that no whole sections have been lost. Now read to note—and eliminate—"typographical errors", mistakes the typesetter has made.

★If possible have more than one person read proof.

By the book method, we use one mark at the point of the error; that we call the "intratype symbol". The symbol that tells the printer how to correct the error is written in the margin. The "marginal symbol" may be written in either margin, but if there is more than one correction symbol for one line, they must be separated by a slash and must always appear in the exact same order as the errors themselves. Thus the marginal symbol for the second error in a line must be the second of such symbols, reading from the left. The first symbol may be in the left margin and the second in the right; both may be in the left or in the right margin, separated by a slash. But in all instances, the symbol for the second error is always second in line.

There are three kinds of typographical errors. The first is when unwanted material appears in type. To delete a single letter, mark a vertical line through it and in the margin write the "delete" sign, a medieval lowercase *d*, which is short for "delendo!". . ."get rid of it!"

If a whole word, or series of words, is to be deleted, mark it out in the type with a single horizontal line. Again, write the delete sign in the margin.

If a letter within a word is deleted, the printer must then "close up" the empty space it leaves. The intratype symbol is the straight line through the offending character; the closeup is shown by little parentheses, lying on their side, at the top and bottom of the strikeout line. In the margin, the delete sign is also enclosed by the little half-moons.

The next broad category of errors is omissions. Here the intratype sign is the "caret", an upside-down *V*, at the point of omission. In the margin, write the character or characters to be inserted.

In case a "superior character" is omitted, the caret is inverted within the type. Superior characters are apostrophes, single and double quotes and those infrequently-used figures such as the *2* in the formula: pi r^2.

To distinguish the apostrophe from the comma, its marginal notation is cradled in an inverted caret. To keep little marginal marks such as punctuation from being overlooked, they are enclosed in a circle or in a regular caret.

Hyphens are called for in the margin with an equal sign to distinguish them from a dash, whose marginal sign is a horizontal line with tiny serifs, or, as some people see it, a very wide and very shallow *H*.

The mark for "space", whether to add it or delete it, is #, the tick-tack-toe device. When space is desired for a paragraph indent,

These symbols .... translate for typesetter into:

ℒ	Delete character(s) marked within type.
Ⓛ	Delete marked character(s) and close up resulting space.
⌒	Remove space between two linked characters.
#	Insert space at point marked by caret.
✓✓✓	Equalize spacing between words throughout entire line.
¶	Begin new paragraph at point marked by L.
no ¶	Don't start new paragraph here. Run all copy into single graf.
⊙	Insert period at caret.
⋏	Insert comma at caret.
⋎	Insert apostrophe at inverted caret.
⋎	Insert quotes at inverted caret.
⋏	Insert inferior figure at caret.
⋎	Insert superior figure at inverted caret.

PROOFREADER'S MARGINAL MARKS tell how to correct errors indicated by intratype symbols. Note confusing similarity to copyreading marks.

2	Insert regular number at caret.
⊢⎯	Insert dash at caret.
=	Insert hyphen at caret.
tr	Transpose characters or words that are joined by lazy-S device.
Ital	Set underlined characters in Italics.
BF	Set underlined characters in boldface.
lc	Change slashed character(s) to lowercase.
cap	Change characters underscored by three lines to capital form.
Out; see copy	So much copy has been left out here, there isn't room to write it in margin. So go back to original copy and set all of it.
QuAu	Author, do you want the "correction" indicated in left of this box?
QuEd	Editor, do you want "correction" indicated in left of this box?
STET	Typesetter, ignore any "corrections" indicated in type but now underlined with dots.

write a capital Sans Serifs *L* where the graf is to start; the marginal symbol is the old, old "paragraph sign", a capital *P* with two legs and facing the opposite way.

The last broad proofreading category is changing an incorrect element to the correct one. The basic intratype mark for changes is to circle the offending element and write the correct one in the margin.

Common exceptions: To change a small letter to a capital, mark three little horizontal and parallel lines under the letter and in the margin write "cap". To change a capital to a small letter, in the type mark through the cap letter with a diagonal slash; the marginal mark is "lc", for lowercase.

When two letters are out of order, a frequent error—"maet" instead of "meat", for instance—the *a* and *e* are looped into an S mark lying on its side and the marginal notation is "tr", for "transpose". The same device is used for words as well.

BOOK METHOD of proof-reading uses intratype symbol to indicate error and marginal symbol for instructions to typesetter. Marks are always used in pairs.

The quick brown fox jumps over the lazy dog.

ꝡ The quick brown foxx jumps over the lazy dog.

ꝡ The quick brown fox jumps over the lazy ~~black~~ dog.

ꝡ The quick brown fox juumps over the lazy dog.

◯ The quick brown fox jum ps over the lazy dog.

The quick brownˌfox jumps over the lazy dog.

ɰ The qṳick brown fox jumps over the lazy dog.

¶ ran away. ⌊The quick brown fox jumps over the

/⬤ The fox jumpsˌquickly and gracefully.

∨ The foxˇs actions were swift and graceful.

∨∨ The fox said,ˇWatch me jump, doggy!"

/2 The fox drinks only H₂O.

2 The quick brown fox ran 3 miles.

= The fox ran helter skelter

⊢ The fox jumps —over the dog to freedom.

u The quick brown fox imps over the lazy dog.

brown The quick fox jumps over the lazy dog.

The fox jumps the dog.   OUT; see copy

brown The quick (grey) fox jumps over the lazy dog.

tr The quick brown fox jumps over the lazy dog.

ital The quick brown fox jumps over the lazy dog.

B.F. The quick brown fox jumps over the lazy dog.

cap the quick brown fox jumps over the lazy dog.

lc The quick brown Fox jumps over the lazy dog.

The quick (grey) fox jumps over the lazy dog. brown STET

c/d The quik brown fox jumps over the lazy dog. tr

⊙ The quick grey fox jumps over the lazy dog

Once in a while we think we're correcting a mistake and find out that we should have kept our cotton-pickin' hands off, that everything was OK the way it was. In that case, within the type, draw a dotted line under the erroneous "correction"; cross out the marginal symbol and, in the margin, write "Stet". This is short for the Latin "stetare"—"let it stand". More inelegantly, it means, "Ooops! I slipped! Please disregard anything I wrote here!"

I am a student at V.C.U. --that's the common term for Virginia Commonwealth University. It is situated in Richmond, Va. As a matter of fact, it is right in downtown Richmond, an urban university in every sense of the term.

While the University was organized within the decade, its roots go back to the last century. The venerable Virginia medical College and the Richmond Technical institute were joined in matrimony; then an arts and Science school was superimposed and the result was a university.

"We are dedicated to the obligation of a truely urban institution," says Dr. Edward Temple, president of the university. We will never have a bucolic campus of romantic academe. But in our city-street setting, we will do our duty as we see it and as our constituents see it."

PROOFREADING done by book method in upper portion, by guideline method in lower part.

26

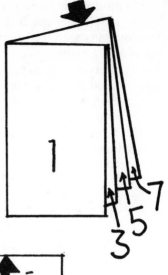

PAGINATION DIAGRAM shows 8-page signature. Arrows indicate "gripper edges" where usually bleeds cannot be printed without unacceptable waste of paper. Sixteen-page signatures are merely folded once more.

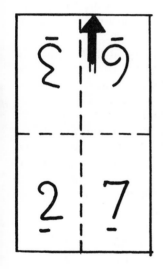 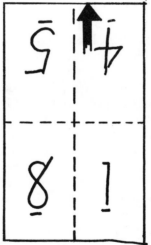

The editor may have the opportunity to correct "page proofs" after the paste-up process has been completed.

★ Make sure that pictures and captions are paired properly.

Mismatching cutlines and photos is all too easy to do. Results are always embarrassing and often verge on libelous.

If you do read page proofs, remember their primary purpose is to see that heads and stories and pix and captions match properly, that margins are consistent and that pages follow in proper order. As these elements have been produced by different people in different parts of the shop, they become separated. Often they are mismatched during pasteup and so the page proof is our chance to check that. We also note that margins are proper and that pages are in proper order.

The book system doesn't work for page proofs. Now we use the "guideline system". The error is circled. From it a line is drawn to the nearest margin (without crossing any other guidelines) and there the regular marginal symbol of the book system is written.

Sometimes a "press proof" is required. This is the first impression from the regular printing press and must be checked in the print shop as the press stands idle—and losing money—while this proofreading is done. Functions of the press proof are to see that the right paper and ink are used and that "signatures" are proper.

Most publications are printed on a belt of paper or on a large sheet that contains at least four pages. This sheet is folded—a signature—and sliced open to create a "book" of several pages. (See sketch and note that pages do not appear in numerical order on a signature. Hence their relative position must be checked at this time.) Again, the guideline system is used.

Proofreading—along with obtaining original copy approval—must be the editor's least-favorite task. The mechanics are tedious and time-consuming. Even worse, though, are the psychological vexations. A column in "The Ragan Report" on this subject brought a host of responses from editors who have suffered through these obstacle courses. So fervent were these responses that it seems worthwhile to reprint that column here:

How do you deal with a boss who, well, is an idiot?

"My one single problem which most concerns me," writes an anonymous respondent, "is to prepare printed jobs for management people who have no journalistic backgrounds and *attempt* to supervise my job assignments. What do I do?"

And here, Gentle Reader, we have one of the ironies of American corporate life. A businessman takes the advice of his accountant, attorney, time-and-motion expert and the elevator operator's mother-in-law. But let a communications person—anyone from editor to advertising director to PR man—throw out a suggestion and it's like throwing out a Christian into the den of lions.

Everyone, but everyone, is an expert in communications. An engineer whose only polysyllabic vocabulary is "sine, cosine," is a literateur in the final analysis. A patent attorney who thinks Zane Grey is American literature, inserts an apostrophe before every final *s* in the copy. A joker who stutters when he answers the telephone complains about the rhythm of the balance sheet and wants a more Elizabethan (Elizabeth Taylor, that is) flavor to the footnote on page 9.

Heaven, as Cynthia Tewsksburreigh was wont to say, help us all!

Unfortunately, the idiots—as the poor—are always among us. More frequently they are a rung or two above us. We can't avoid them (it would be a lonely world if all the idiots were removed) so we must learn to live with them.

The first thing is to translate everything possible into $ and ¢. This is usually the most telling criterion for these incorporated Mickey Mousers. Have those financial data at your fingertips. If Maximus T. Bloughard insists on green paper for your Christmas issue, have a sample of Novatone Heather, 80-pound substance ready to show him.

"Oh yes," you interject, "I thought you'd like something like this. Your favorite shade of green as I recall. But, alas, this will add $196.47 to the bill and I'll need to ask you to authorize this request for a budget exception."

How salutary a phrase. . ."budget exception"!

You know what Wordsworth Q. Pepperpincher is going to say— well ahead of the very confrontation. For he is as programmed as Pavlov's dogs. Have an alternative ready—with its price tag, of course—for any objection Mr. P might raise.

The next defensive ploy is the deadline.

Before any job, make a pact with the president's secretary. "Shall we say, then, that I'll have the material for Mr. Bigg's attention on February 12?"

To this she can only say yes.

Now when Phinella Hayersplittier starts suggesting rewriting the Old Testament, gently interject the deadline with the president into the conversation. "I'd like to do this, Ms. H," you gently submit, "but I'll get in dutch with the Big Man. Would you give a buzz to his secretary and get me an extension. You carry more weight with him (she sure does, 225 pounds) than I do."

Filthy lucre rears its head here again. Arrange with your printer (who at heart is as much an anarchist as any editor) that on a certain date, overtime rates set in on your job. He need not be too intent on levying said rates. But it is very handy to explain to one of the hierarchical vultures that his or her suggestion will set up past March 11. . ."and that's the overtime rate date, you know."

Another moment of extreme vulnerability for an editor is when he must show proofs.

The saving device here is the Xerox. Never submit the original printer's proof. Always give a photocopy to the harpies. This has several benefits.

First of all, photocopier paper isn't pleasant to write on. Its surface is too glassy.

Secondly, each person is proofing only one, personal copy. There's no chance for one-upmanship. This is a major factor in extensive author's alterations.

Sales Manager J. reads the proof first. He makes a few obvious corrections, simple typos. Then he bucks it on to Personnel Supervisor W. She has no obvious corrections to make. But. . . .

"I'll show that smart-bottomed Jack Jones that I'm as smart as he is. Hand me my red pencil and let me at it!"

And, because there aren't any typographical errors to mark, she changes "red" to "crimson" and "fire" to "conflagration," etc., and you're stuck with two extra days and a hundred bucks worth of AAs.

There's another factor in a communal proof. Otherwise placid and peaceful executives are like a school of piranhas. They get drunk on blood. As they see the wounds of previous proofreaders' marks, our heroes become as maddened as the carnivorous fish. Each correction is a stigmatum, discharging the intoxicating serum. The fewer previous "corrections," the less the blood lust.

One editor I know affixes a memo to each proof:

"Please read this proof before _____. At

that time your corrections will be combined on the master proof of Mr. President. Because of budgetary considerations, you are reminded that our printer goes into overtime rates _____ and that each alteration on this proof costs $3.73."

If you combine the various "corrections" onto the master proof yourself, you can always leave one out. "I noticed that Mr. Bigg had approved this statement (He hadn't; he had merely not disapproved!) and I was sure you wouldn't want to contradict him," you might observe casually.

Or you may just—most sincerely—plead human error on your part. But chances are you have to do neither. Most alleged "corrections" are mere gambits in the executive-wing game and are forgotten before you even send the proof back to the composing room.

Another important tactic of editorial self-preservation is: "Never ask for permission."

An Army editor (it was me, in fact) once told a general, "It's easier to get forgiveness for something you've done in this division than it is to get permission to do it." That applies to most commercial armies, too, I've found.

Do it. If it succeeds, praise your bosses. (One of them must have, back last Spring or a year or so ago, said something that could be construed as the embryo for any brilliant idea ever hatched.) If it doesn't work, ask forgiveness.

Finally, collect character witnesses.

Every time you win a contest, make very, very sure that your officers' ranks are made aware of that. Pass along—and keep for your files—kind words from practitioners in your field. Display your plaques and certificates prominently and proudly.

You are your own best character reference. The capable editor has an air about him or her that comes only from self-confidence. That comes only from complete mastery of your subject.

I know that this little screed sounds sophist and cynical. It wasn't meant to be. Each ploy given here is a legitimate one. It may be a wee bit childish to you. But when you're playing with 3-foot-high people, you play dolls and Fish, not Monopoly and contract bridge.

* * * *

It's wise to make a little, sketchy "pagination" to show how pages pair up. In an 8-page publication page 2 and 7 are on the same plate; in a 16-pager, page 2 pairs with 15. If more than two pages are printed in a single signature, sheet, placement of pages is a bit trickier and needs close checking.

★ Avoid all AAs except those required to correct factual errors.

Typographical errors are those made by the printer; he must correct them at his own cost. But when the editor has second thoughts and alters type that has been set correctly, we call it an "author's alteration" or "AA". Guess who pays for those? Right! The editor. And the cost is high.

Print shops may modify proofreading practices. But those described here, and the symbols shown in the accompanying sketch, are standard ones. If you use them, any typesetter will be able to follow your instructions and purge the printed page of all error.

★ Initial every proof after you've read it.

Proofreading is the only graphic arts product that the practitioner autographs. This is not to further suicidal impulses and set up the proofreader as the fall guy should an error go undetected. Just the opposite; it goes back to the 1400's when proofreading first began and was a mark of pride, an attesting that the proofreader knew how important this process was, that the best job possible had been done and that the corrector was proud of it.

Proofs may be marked "OK/JG" which means that it is free of errors, "clean". (A "dirty proof" has nothing to do with pornography; it's simply one with many errors.)

Marking a proof "OK/WC–JG" means that errors have been noted. But if the typesetter follows each correction as shown on the proof, the result will be acceptable. "JG", of course, are the proofreader's initials.

★ Always note the difference between proofreader's marks and those of the copyreader.

The copyreader or editor uses marks much like those of the proofreader. These marks are close enough in appearance to create confusion but are still different enough to wreak havoc if either set of symbols are used for the opposite process.

Now comes what most editors consider the most fun of all:

"Dummying up" the publication.

"Dummy" is a verb, to design a plan that the printer follows in putting together a page. It is also a noun, that blueprint itself. (And many an editor has other, more pungent uses for the word.)

Dummies are most conveniently drawn on preprinted sheets. Most common are 8½ x 11 in size. Along one or both sides are tick-marks in increments used by the editor. These may be inches or BLs; if the latter, they are usually in about 1-inch groupings or by 5's or 10's.

Dummy sheets are not drawn to scale; they are almost always wider than in actual proportion.

Instructions to the printer or pasteup department are given in symbols for the sake of speed and saving space.

★ The depth of each element must be given in the smallest possible unit of measurement.

Heads are indicated by their slugline and the code that shows their size and variety. (A chart showing the BLs for every head you use should be made a constant reference.)

Body type is shown by a straight line that runs down the middle of the column on the dummy. As head and story should have the same slugline, only that of the head need be written out.

★ Indicate the start of a story by an asterisk.

If a story wraps from one column to another, a diagonal line runs from the end of one leg of type to the top of the next.

★ An arrowhead indicates the end of a story.

A picture is designated by a rectangle crossed by diagonals. Any rules—elements that print lines—are drawn in heavily and are described in the margin. A "hairline" might be the designation of a "cutoff rule"; that for a box might be marked as "6-point Oxford rule" or, more frequently, by the serial number of the rule as used by the printer: "Rule No. 7", etc.

Flatout material—described later in the body-type section—and the use of color elements are also designated in the margins.

★ The pasteup dummy is the most precise.

For this dummy, pasteup sheets of the exact size are used. All copy, heads and body, is photocopied. Then every element is pasted into the desired position, allowing precisely the proper amount of space between elements.

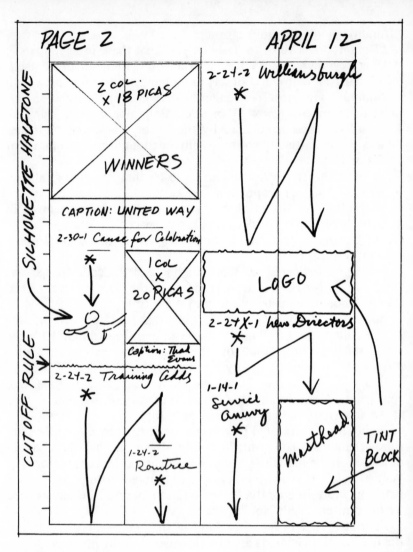

SKETCH DUMMY for newspaper page shows start of story with asterisk and end by arrow. Pictures are designated by diagonal crosses; any unusual device by wavy line and marginal instructions. Note that straight line at end of story is merely to indicate its length, not cutoff rule. Cutoff is shown by wavy line.

...NEWSPAPER PAGE created by following dummy. Minor adjustments are made during pasteup process.

Pictures, in the size to which they have been reduced—not their original size—are either drawn in as rectangles or are represented by properly-sized pieces of construction paper or even Photostats.

The printer will follow a pasteup dummy precisely and so the dummy must provide "justified columns", those of exactly the same length as all others.

If the editor furnishes pasteups to the printer, the finished product is the same as the pasteup dummy except that the original cold type is used.

No matter where the pasteups are done there is a temptation to clip material from a previous issue to paste up. If this happens, the resultant reproduction will be fuzzy; if this material in turn is again used for pasting up, soon the image will be dirty and look like worn hot type.

★ Insist on camera-fresh copy for finished pasteups, "mechanicals".

If, as in the case of many editors, you do not see page proofs, the pasteup dummy or final pasteup should be scrutinized closely as the final proofreading step.

★ Establish realistic deadlines; then keep them zealously.

Work out production deadlines with the printer. Be sure that these are realistic. For instance, don't set the printer's delivery of proofs at 4:30 Friday afternoon and your return thereof at 9 Monday morning. . . .unless you intend to work over the weekend. If bosses must OK proofs, count in that dead time. Be sure not to overlook holidays, especially long ones.

All other deadlines, from accepting contributions through all the editorial procedures, must be based on the printer's schedule requirements.

★ Deadlines are sacred.

Of course deadlines must be bent on occasion. No editor will start the press while the Titanic is sinking! But there are many stories of far less consequence that ought not hold up presstime. Make exceptions to deadlines on a commonsensical basis. . . .and keep those exceptions rare.

As soon as the finished publication comes from the printer read it carefully for typographic errors—they do sneak by—and put only corrected copies in your files. Also note anything unusual about the issue—a substituted paper, a new ink, a special screen used for a halftone, etc. This will save much head-scratching should similar circumstances arise.

No one has ever insisted that the mechanical processes of getting a publication to press are delirious fun. Often, even in the best of conditions, the work is tedious and even monotonous. But well-planned procedures, followed meticulously, will minimize the discomfort and allow the maximum of the editor's time, energy and attention to be devoted to the purely creative parts of the job.

2

Body Type

Body type is the meat and potatoes around which your whole typographic menu must be planned. It's far more important than many editors realize.

★ Choose a body type with a large x-height.

Although type size is designated in points, that specification is not very precise. You must, with your own eye, determine that the size is adequate. The "x-height" is the distance between the bottom of "primary letters" such as *a, m, o* and *x* and their top. Usually a face with a large x-size has relatively short "ascenders"– the necks on the letters like b, d and h—and "descenders"—the tails on g, p, q, etc.

★ You can see a pumpkin easier than a goose-egg.

That's the printer's way of saying that greatest readability comes from faces that are based on a circle rather than an oval. So inspect all letters with "bowls"–a, b, c, g, o, etc.—and make sure the circular portion is truly circular.

★ Ledd adequately.

"Ledding"–also spelled "leading"–is the extra space between lines. There's no formula for this function. Generally speaking, 7- through 9-point type can take either a half-point or full-point of ledding. Again the editor's own eye must decide the proper amount.

Set a block of 20 lines to determine if ledding is adequate.

★ Set body type as close as possible to the optimum line length.

The "optimum line length" is 38 to 42 characters.

★ Keep line lengths within the readability range.

The minimum line length that we can expect a reader to consume with comfort is 30 characters; the maximum is 60.

If you stay within two or three characters of any of these specifications, you'll be serving your reader well.

★ A more sophisticated formula is:

$$O = lca \times 1\frac{1}{2}$$
$$Mn = O - 25\%$$
$$Mx = O + 50\%$$

O is the "optimum line length".

Each font of type has its own "lca", "lowercase alphabet length". This is simply all the little letters, a through z, set in one line and measured in points.

The specific lca, times 1½, gives the optimum line length in points.

As we must designate line lengths in printer's measurements—1 point equals 1/72 inch; 12 points equal 1 pica—we must then count out at least 20 lines of the type in question to determine the

READABILITY RANGE for each typeface used by publication is shown in wall chart for handy reference. Here Caledonia is used for body type, 10-point Techno for caption material and Techno Bold for tabular matter.

TYPE RANGES

Caledonia 10pt Mn 12¼ OP 16¼ Mx 24

Techno 10pt Mn 10¾ OP 14½ Mx 22

Techno Bld. 6pt Mn 8 OP 11¼ Mx 16

average length of 40 characters. The width difference of skinny *l, t,* and *i* must be averaged off against the fatso *m* and *w*.

Once the optimum, *O*, has been determined, we can readily find *Mn*, the minimum, and *Mx*, the maximum, which are the boundaries of the "readability range".

You ought to determine these three specifications for each body face you use . . . then stay within the boundaries.

★ It is possible to have too-large body type.

Should you choose a large body size, you may well find that the column-width dictated by your paper width will allow far fewer characters than the minimum.

Metropolitan newspapers sometimes emphasize important stories by setting the lead paragraphs in a larger body type and in wider measure. For publications editors, however, this practice isn't worth the trouble and extra expense it occasions.

If such treatment is used, the break from wide to narrower measure and from large to small type should not happen at the same time. Instead of going from "2-column, 12-point" type to "1-column, 8-point", go from "2-column, 12" to "1-column, 12," then "1-column, 8." Or you can go from "2-column, 12" to "2-column, 8," then "1-column, 8."

In all instances, make sure that the readability range is observed.

★ Avoid runarounds.

When the width of a column of type is narrowed, then resumed, to create an opening into which is placed a small "pork-chop", a portrait, or some other typographic element, a "runa-round" has been formed.

This is not a good practice. It disturbs the reading rhythm, obviously, and the narrow lines usually are far under the readability range.

★ Body type should be set flush left and right.

We've already noted the function of the A/O (in the previous chapter) which dictates flush-left setting. When we must do a highly repetitive task, it is physically and mentally more pleasant if we can do it rhythmically. Therefore when we make all lines of equal length—by "justifying type", setting with straight left and right margins—we assure against constantly-changing line lengths

RUNAROUND is formed by lines shortened to make opening for picture (as here), logo or other type. Such a change breaks reading rhythm.

which disconcert the eye.

TWEET! TWEET! That's the whistle that says, "Wait a minute! Justified type is the best for readability. But if for any valid reason you must set type ragged right, go ahead!" [Note the glossary in this book.]

It's better to communicate with 100% of your potential audience at an esthetic level of 75% than to maintain a 100% level of esthetics but reach only 50% of your potential audience.

So, if time or budget dictates a little lower level of esthetics, it's better to use what's available than not to communicate at all.

With conventional phototypesetting, there is no economic advantage in setting unjustified type. The computer does the justification and it's there whether or not you use it. But if you're "setting" your own type by "strikeon" methods, justification does take more time. But. . . .

★ It's worth the time and effort to justify strikeon composition.

"Strikeon composition" is that done by a typewriter-like machine. The simplest, of course, is the portable Corona in your den. The most sophisticated has an inboard computer that justifies lines automatically.

It isn't too hard to justify ordinary typewritten matter, though. The accompanying diagram shows how simple it is.

Electric typewriters are best for homemade typesetting—whether for pasteup or to cut Mimeograph stencils—as they have a uniform stroke for every character. Be sure that your typewriter is clean before you start and clean it again at the end of every two pages of typing. A good ribbon is, of course, essential.

★ Don't set type in decorative shapes.

Especially at Christmastime, every editor is tempted to use type ornamentally, to set it in the shape of a Yule tree or bell or something other than a rectangle. The result is rarely happy from an esthetic viewpoint and from a mechanical—and hence financial—angle it's sheer extravagance.

★ Body type should be Roman.

Tests show that the reader can read the Roman race more quickly, easily, comfortably and several other ly's as well, with less fatigue and greater comprehension.

★ Sans Serifs have low readability.

Because Sans Serifs are crisp and clean and give a modern feeling, artists love them. But by profession, picture people are not much concerned with words. Thus they're willing to sacrifice readability—if they even consider it—for appearance. The editor, however, must make readability the major criterion of all body type.

A good compromise is Optima, variously known as Chelmsford, Oracle or other monikers—each manufacturer gives it a different name.

★ Optima has good readability.

Optima is a Roman face with the serifs removed. Its modulated strokes give adequate readability; lack of serifs give a clarity that art directors like.

★ Sans Serifs are good for captions.

Descriptive matter for pictures is called "captions" in magazines and "cutlines" in newspapers, and "caption material" in both. The Sans are good for this use; readability is high enough for the relatively few words in captions. Also, the letterform is distinctive enough so it will not be confused with surrounding body type.

★ Avoid Italic body type in masses.

The lighter tone of the Italic form seems to scare away prospective readers who feel it is going to be difficult to read . . . although actually it isn't.

"Editor's notes" are often set in Italic. Not only should this setting be avoided, the notes themselves ought to be eliminated. Reporters are always told: "Don't back into a story; jump into it!" An editor's note merely delays the reader from jumping into the story.

```
        To "justify" typewritten material, draw a line
   at the desired measure. When the line is short,xx
   fill it out with x's. Then put in check marksxxxx
   where the extra space will go in the finished re-
   typing. After a period or comma is the best place
   but try to avoid extra space after an l.

        If your typewriter enables you to squeeze in a
   letter in a half space, if you run beyond the line      (1)
   write the number in excess in the right marginxxx
   The best place to squeeze up is after an l or ixx
   or after a punctuation mark.

        If you can't half-space and you go over thexxx
   ~~mark, simply cross out the line that's too long and~~
   mark, simply cross out the line that's too longxx
   and type it again, shorter.
```

JUSTIFICATION METHOD for type "set" on typewriter produces. . . .

Material in such notes can usually be included in the story itself, down in the third or fourth graf, or in a "bio note", a short graf about the author and, especially, his qualifications to pass judgment on the subject of the piece, which runs at the foot of the page.

★ Avoid large masses of boldface.

Six or seven lines of boldface should be the maximum ever used in one area, except in a sideless box.

★ Avoid boldface read-ins.

The practice of starting a paragraph—or captions—with a few words set in bold caps, then reverting to lightface lowercase, is a "read-in". Not only non-functional, it's definitely malfunctional.

To "justify" typewritten material, draw a line at the desired measure. When the line is short, fill it out with x's. Then put in check marks where the extra space will go in the finished re-typing. After a period or comma is the best place but try to avoid extra space after an $\underline{1}$**.**

If your typewriter enables you to squeeze in a letter in a half space, if you run beyond the line write the number in excess in the right margin. The best place to squeeze up is after an $\underline{1}$ **or** $\underline{i}$ **or after a punctuation mark.**

If you can't half-space and you go over the mark, simply cross out the line that's too long and type it again, shorter.

. . .this justified copy. Longer
lines require less manipulation
than short ones.

★ Never start a story with boldface.

★ Avoid reverses of body type.

A "reverse plate" gives the effect of white type on a black (or colored) background. Reversed type is difficult to read. If type must be reversed, it should be no smaller than 10-point and, preferably, Sans Serifs. When Roman is reversed, there's a tendency for the thin strokes and serifs to plug up with ink.

Reverses should be on black or full color. White letters on gray or a tint are difficult to see.

★ Use tint blocks warily.

Tint blocks are areas of color or gray on which type or art is surprinted. Gray areas diminish "visibility", which depends on contrast between the type and its background. Thus readability is also diminished. The darker the gray background, the lower readability.

If color is used as a tint block, it must be "screened down", peppered with tiny white dots to make a "tint" of the original shade. Only yellow can be used effectively in its full value as a tint block. Red must be screened down to pink, navy blue to robin-egg blue, etc.

When you do use a tint block, treat it like a "little page". Be sure that there are adequate margins all around the page of tone, just as there are around a page of paper.

A continuing problem is avoiding large, gray masses of body type, as uninviting as a bowl of yesterday's cold oatmeal.

★ Use the dollar gauge.

When a dollar bill is placed horizontally on a page, it should always touch at least one display element—head, art or a box. If it doesn't, there is too great a concentration of gray, unappetizing body type.

★ Use breaker heads.

The only way to break such a mass is with a "breaker head". This has the content of the old "subhead". But while that subhead was set in bold caps of body type, the breaker is in 12-, 14- or even 18-point headletter, flush left.

The breaker looks like a headline and its first effect is to break up a long story into several apparently short ones, as the reader is always more ready to jump into a short piece.

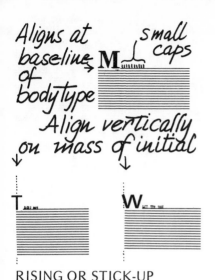

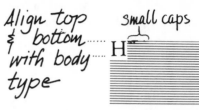

RISING OR STICK-UP
INITIALS

INSET OR SUNKEN INITIALS. If available in body type, small capitals are usually used for about 10 characters following initials.

★ Use stickup initials.

"Decorative initials" are useful for breaking up masses of type in magazine format. "Inset" or "sunken initials" are dropped into the top-left corner of a block of type. Ideally they should align at the top with the top of the first line of body type and at the bottom with the baseline of adjacent body type. This is difficult and often practically impossible to achieve.

The "rising" or "stickup" initial aligns only with the baseline of the first line of body type. This is easy to do. A side benefit is the built-in area of white space alongside the rising initial.

It is an amenity, but not essential, that after a decorative initial, the following word or phrase—about a third of the line length—is set in capitals. Be sure that the change from caps to lowercase does not awkwardly break the meaning of that phrase.

Never, SEN. JOHN A. Case, or NEWARK, NEW Jersey!

★ Use horizontal layout.

When body type is arranged in horizontal instead of vertical areas, its mass seems smaller. As the reader is scared away by large areas of gray type—and more willing to jump into short stories—it's advantageous to use type in wide, shallow rectangles.

Dogleg {

DOGLEG is any column breaking out of a rectangle of body type. It is often used to prevent tombstoning below horizontally displayed copy.

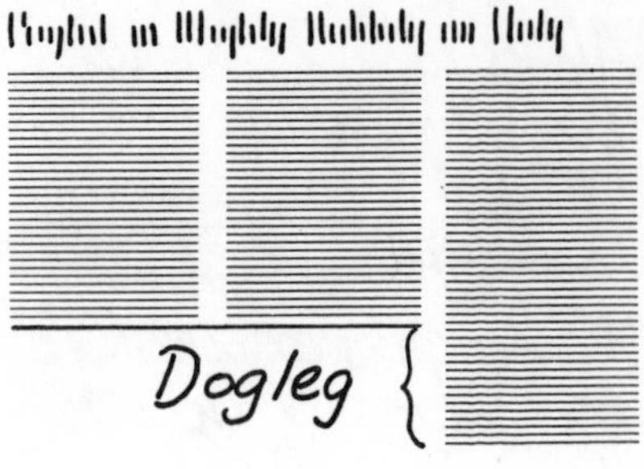

★ Horizontal type need not be squared off at the bottom.

If type must be stepped at the bottom to meet other makeup conditions, the protruding "dogleg" should be kept as short as reasonably possible.

★ Use flatout material.

"Flatout" matter is also called "1-up". One more column of space is used than there are columns of type. So, we'd put four columns of type across five columns of space, or use "3-across-4". (Two-across-3 doesn't work well.)

The extra column of space is used to enlarge the alleys between type.

Typically, for a paper using 11-pica columns and 1-pica alleys, specs for 4-across-5 would be:

    4 picas space
    Leg of type
    4 picas #
    Type
    4 picas #
    Type
    4 picas #
    Type
    3 picas #

Note that the new alleys are not always of the same width. If there is irregularity, make the last alley the narrowest or don't add any space to it—the normal alley will be there anyway. The first alley—which is, of course, in addition to the normal 1-pica alley at the left—may also be narrowed or even eliminated.

46

ONE-UP, also called flatout, uses one more column of space than legs of type. Type is set at regular measure and extra column widens alleys between legs. Head aligns flush left with first leg. Note here that alleys are not equal to space at ends of flatout and that left margin is greater than right.

This 1-up form is 3-across-4

★ The editor should spec flatout matter, never leave it to the printer.

The editor should prepare specifications for 3-across-4, 4-across-5 or, for a broadsheet, 5-6, 6-7 and 7-8.

★ Use Canadian wraps on long stories.

With this technique—a variation on horizontal layout—a 2- or 4-column head is used. The story starts in the first column and

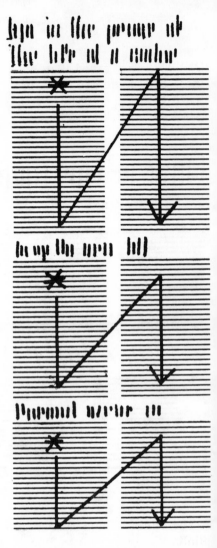

CANADIAN WRAP arranges 1-column type in 2-column segments under a multicolumn head, using 2-column breaker heads.

runs about 4 to 5 inches deep, then wraps over into the second column.

A 2-column breaker head is dropped below this 2-column portion and the body type continues, wrapped into two columns again. The wrap is repeated till the whole story has been placed.

(See sketch.)

The effect is to break a large, unappetizing mass of type into smaller, bitable portions. This technique is good for handling a lengthy report, presidential message, company statement, etc.

★ Use pepper to mark itemization.

"Pepper" is little spots of typographic color such as "bullets"— large periods, black or open squares, check marks, etc. It is used to signal the start of a new item in a list of such materials.

(Numbers may be used, of course, in the same way, ticking off a variety of points. But numbers suggest a set of priorities that often do not exist and pepper is better for such more-random listing.)

When a pepper device is used, customarily we do not indent a paragraph.

★ Don't let tabular material fall apart.

If you have to list material in two or more columns, be sure that the space between them is no wider than 12 to 15 characters. Never set:

| Minnesota | 85% |
| Arizona | 79% |

etc. Instead, move the columns within 10 spaces, thus:

| Minnesota | 85% |
| Arizona | 79% |

etc. Or use "leaders", a line of dots or dashes, thus:

Minnesota 85%
Arizona 79%

or

Minnesota – – – – – – – 85%
Arizona– – – – – – – – 79%

etc.

★ Use sideless boxes.

"Sideless boxes" give a little extra zip to body type. They are made by using some kind of "decorative rule" at the top and bottom only. Body type is set boldface, for the extra color it gives, and the head is short and centered, in the accent headletter if possible.

Sideless boxes may be in one or two columns. But they should never be deeper than 3 inches. Two-column boxes may have the body type indented 2 picas on each side, with the rules in full 2-column width.

★ Keep sandwiches short.

A "sandwich" is a small sideless box without a head. It is usually used for a "reefer", a line or two that refers the reader to associated stories on another page. Sandwiches should not be deeper than three lines, preferably two.

A pica of white space should run above and below a box and 6 points of space between the rules and the head or story. A sandwich takes 6 points space above and below with no extra space within the rules.

★ Don't worry about widows.

This is purely typographical—not a sociological or even social—admonition. A "widow" is a short line of type at the end of a paragraph. Just how short is a matter of debate. Some experts say any line shorter than a half or a third full is a widow; others insist anything at all less than full should be so termed.

Try to avoid extremely short widows at the top or bottom of a column. Especially avoid a short line such as the portion of a hyphenated word at the top of a column. The reader feels cheated to have to carry the hyphen way to the next column, then find only that tiny fragment of a word up there.

★ Don't try to square off caption material.

Magazine editors, especially, often try to make captions into neat rectangles. This usually requires adding extra words or deleting some to avoid the widow. Usually this mars the smooth flow of words and it certainly isn't worth the trouble and expense of resetting type. Extremely short widows may be eliminated by deleting a previous word or two. Try to keep such alterations in the second-last line, if at all possible, to reduce the cost of author's alterations.

Just remember that body type carries the overwhelming portion of the information in your publication. Use plain common sense in presenting body type in the most easy and convenient way possible.

3

Headlines

Headlines are the most conspicuous elements on a page and so their strengths and weaknesses are also most apparent.

There are two kinds of headlines, defined by content. "Summary" or "definitive" heads are those in typical newspaper style: MAN BITES DOG. "Connotative" or "teaser" heads pique the curiosity of the reader by hinting, rather than summarizing, the content of its story. On our human/canine account, a teaser head might say HOG DOG WITHOUT MUSTARD. (Note that headlines are set in all caps in this text merely to distinguish them from body type. In actual usage, as we'll soon see, all-cap setting is to be shunned.)

★ Follow the grammar of headlines.

Headlines are written in a language all their own . . . and with grammatical rules all their own. Although the reader is unfamiliar with these formal rules, a grammatical violation discomforts him. He has subconsciously learned proper grammar from reading newspapers.

★ Heads are written in the historical present tense.

COMPANY SETS
SALES RECORD

means that the company did so yesterday.

Only when the pluperfect is needed do we write heads in the conventional past tense. Future is indicated by the infinitive.

means that a record set long before yesterday has just been disclosed or discovered.

COMPANY TO SET
SALES RECORDS

means that it will do so tomorrow.

★ Omit articles and conjunctions.

A comma takes the place of "and"; a semicolon is the equivalent of a period. "The", "a" and "an" are never used.

★ Omit forms of "to be" in the passive voice.

We don't, in headlines, say JONES IS ELECTED. It's simply JONES ELECTED.

Although a headline is a sentence, periods are never used. Where a period would be used in normal text matter, in a headline a semicolon takes its place:

FIRE RAZES FACTORY; ALL WORKERS FURLOUGHED

★ Headlines should have only one thought.

A semicolon shows that at least two thoughts are connected. So a semicolon is a signal to examine the head. One thought might be eliminated, stressing only the major one. Or the two may be combined into a single sentence:

WORKERS FURLOUGHED AFTER FIRE RAZES FACTORY

Single quotation marks are used instead of the conventional double ones. A colon often introduces a person quoted or sets the stage as to time or place of an action.

JOHNSON: 'ENERGY CRISIS LOOMS'
ALABAMA: HIGHEST IN SALES CONTEST
1997: AIR WILL BE 100% PURE

★ Abbreviations in heads should be used only in titles.

We may say, JONES MFG. CO. but never TWO MFG. COS. TO MERGE. We might have, in the latter example, have said, 2 COMPANIES, etc. An old injunction against starting a head with a number has been eroded. Words are still preferred to numbers from a visual point of view but numbers are not absolutely forbidden any more.

In heads, as in text type, we combine words and numbers as in $5 MILLION or even 25 THOUSAND.

★ Because headlines are read line for line, they must be written that way, too.

The classic example of breaking a closely-linked thought from one line of a head to another is:

SOVIET VIRGIN
LANDS SHORT
OF GOAL AGAIN

Note how far the translation of this head is from the meaning it seeks to convey:

SOVIET
VIRGIN LANDS
(ARE) SHORT
OF GOAL AGAIN

★ Avoid imperative heads.

"Imperative" or "admonitory" heads are those without a subject:

EAT SPOILED FOOD IN JAIL

A reader with any taste at all will respond with, "No, thanks; I have my own restaurant and it's not the jail."

★ Headlines should be simple in form.

In Civil War days, headlines went on and on, often filling half a column. Now by applying the criteria of functionalism, American editors have generally eliminated second and third "decks" on headlines. This simplification gets the reader into the meat of body type more quickly.

★ Headlines should be large in size.

While the typical publication will not need, nor want, the blaring head sizes of the "National Star", its editor must be sure that heads generally are large enough to avoid a typographic monotone pitched at a soporific tone level.

A line of 48 point is worth more than two lines of 24. We should always seek the largest size that is appropriate to the worth of a story and is compatible with the personality of our publication.

★ Heads grade stories by importance.

We gauge heads against two scales. The most important story of a given issue gets the largest headline . . . of that issue. But there is a continuing scale also. If the big story this issue is on the addition of a $125,000 wing on a building, it will not get as big a head as did a $20 million contract story in the last issue. The editor must always have a Walking-on-Water head in reserve for a truly epochal story . . . even though the expectations of such a great event are mighty slim.

Just as the decibel rating of a sport jacket tells us something

SPACING CHART shows proper spacing for all typographic arrangements. Note that chart is not in proportion.

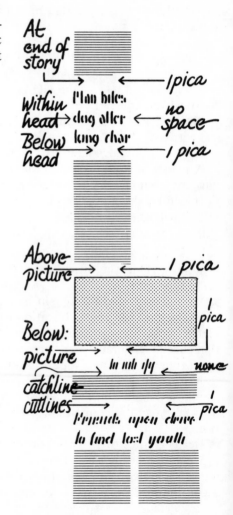

about the man who wears it, so the noise level of headlines indicates the personality of a publication. We need only look at the funereal pages of the "New York Times" in contrast to those of the "National Enquirer" to see this principle demonstrated.

★ All heads should be written flush left.

The constant reaction of the reader, to return to the axis of orientation after reading any line, prompts us to start the succeeding line right on the A/O where we know the reader will be waitin' and ready to start.

★ Head spacing must be consistent.

A written "spec sheet" should show all spacing within and around a head, between it and the story above, between its lines, between the head and its own story.

★ Do not ledd headlines.

The normal spacing between lines of headletters is not only adequate, it's close to ideal. Don't expand this spacing.

Inter-line spacing should be measured from the baseline of the top line to the meanline of the lower one. This spacing should always be the same whether or not there are ascenders or descenders in either line.

★ Word spacing in heads should be one en.

An "en" is half the point size, in width, of the headletter. So a 24-point head should have half of 24—12 points—spacing between words. This should not be changed—especially not reduced—to make the head fit.

★ Heads should be written ragged-right.

The irregular right silhouette is appealing to the reader. If each line of the head comes into the last leg of type, it's long enough. It doesn't matter whether the first, second or third line is the longer or longest.

★ Underscoring runs under descenders.

Never break an underscore to allow descenders to project. This is time-consuming, looks fussy and is harder to read.

★ All heads should be set downstyle.

In "downstyle", only the first word of a sentence or head and proper nouns are capitalized. This follows the capping practice for body type, the composition most read by anyone and most familiar, therefore.

Avoid the bastardization of downstyle in which proper nouns are set lowercase. It is as much a misspelling to write "january" as it is to spell it "Yanuary".

In English correct usage, all proper nouns are capped. Lowercasing denigrates "John Smith", a proper noun, a specific person, to "john smith", a craftsman who specializes in toilets!

★ Avoid all-cap heads.

YOU CAN TEST THE LEGIBILITY OF ALL-CAP HEADS BY SIMPLY TYPEWRITING A PARAGRAPH COMPLETELY IN UPPER-CASE LETTERS. THESE LETTERS ARE HARD TO READ BECAUSE WE DISTINGUISH WORDS PRIMARILY BY THEIR UPPER SILHOUETTE AND, IN ALL CAPS, THAT'S A NON-DISTINCTIVE STRAIGHT LINE.

As You Can Again Determine Yourself, Heads Set In Upper-And-Lower Style Are Much Easier to Read. That's Why For A Couple Generations, This Was The Standard Headline Style.

But downstyle—the style you're reading right now—is by far the easiest to read. And if that's not enough reason to change, it's also easier to write and to set.

★ One-column heads should be no deeper than three lines but can go to four if short words are used.

★ Multicolumn heads should run no deeper than two lines.

★ If a second deck is used, it should be at least two lines deep and have at least as many lines as the main head.

★ The maximum characters and spaces in a headline is 45.

★ The maximum characters and spaces in a single line of a head is 32.

So a 1-line head can have no more than 32 characters but a 3-line head could have 15 characters in each line.

An extra character or two won't be fatal. But exceeding this maximum by any substantial amount will result in a pedestrian, plodding head, totally lacking in immediacy, action and reader-appeal.

For this measurement, all characters count alike. But when we "count a headline" to see if it will fit, we use "units" rather than characters because—especially in display sizes—the difference between a skinny *l* or *f* and the chubby *M* or *W* is so marked we can't use one measurement for both.

★ Count headlines precisely.

The standard unit is the normal lowercase letter such as *a, b, c,* etc. Each of these letters counts 1.

★ Flitjays count ½.

In all fonts the *l* and *i* are narrow and in most fonts the *f, t* and *j* are also skinny. Hence the term "flitjays". The editor must, of course, determine which of the flitjays are ½-counters in each specific headline font!

★ Wammies count 1½.

"Wammies" are, of course, the *w* and *m.*

★ Capital letters count 1½. The exception is *I* which is only 1 and *M* and *W* which are 2. Space between words counts ½.

Some editors build in a safety factor by counting all lowercase letters as 1, all caps as 2, the flitjays as 1, the capital wammies as 3 and space between words as 1.

It doesn't matter which method you use as long as you determine the maximum units per line by that method and you use only that one method.

★ Use bimos for variety.

"Bimos"—pronounced buy-moe and short for "bimodular"—have two elements, a main head and a supportive one.

The most common is the "kicker". The kicker is half the point size of the main head, set flush left and underscored. It should be written no longer than one third the overall width of the headline area. The main head is indented about 10% of the total width. To make it easier, we usually specify "1 pica indent per column" for ordinary newspaper columns of 10 to 12 picas, or 1½ picas per column when wider measures are used.

The "reverse kicker" is also called a "hammer" because of its great impact on a page. Now the kicker is twice the point size of the main head. Set flush left, it is underscored and written no wider than half the overall head width. The main head is indented about 20%, twice the per-column indent under a conventional kicker.

★ Under both kinds of kickers, the main head is most effective with two lines.

★ Kickers should not run at the top of the page; hammers should not run at any margin.

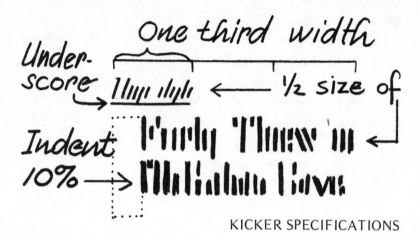

KICKER SPECIFICATIONS

Ignoring this rule means the white space built around the kickers merely dilutes the margins.

The "wicket" and the "tripod" are the next pair. The wicket is two lines of small type set flush *right*. Then comes 1 pica of space and the main head, in twice the point size of the wicket.

The tripod reverses the arrangement. It's a single short line of larger type as a bimo element, then, after 1 pica space, a 2-line main head.

★Wickets and tripods should be written either in ½- or 1½-column widths.

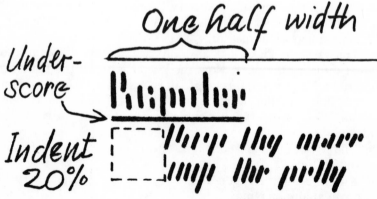

HAMMER SPECIFICATIONS

1 pica space ➔ **Make this at least 50% wider than bimo**

Keep this break away from alley

WICKET (top) AND TRIPOD SPECIFICATIONS. 1-pica space between bimo and main head should come as close as possible to center of body-type column. It must be separated from alley to avoid appearance of tombstoned heads.

This is to prevent the space between the elements from coming at or near the alley between columns of body type.

★ The main head in wickets or tripods should always be at least twice as long as the bimo.

★ Usually the bimo is Italic to a Roman main head or vice versa.

The last bimo, the "slash head", is used mostly for magazines. It consists of a diagonal rule, top-right to lower left. Aligned at the top and at its left is a wicket and, 1 pica lower and to the right of the slash, a 2-line main head. This is an interesting head that gives much dynamic thrust to a page.

★ Avoid chopped heads.

A chopped head has a second and/or third line that is narrower than the first line by at least one column. Body type runs in that vacant column.

★ Avoid jammed heads.

There are two kinds of "jammed heads". A "tombstone" is when two heads are side by side horizontally. The 'stone can be broken only by moving one of the heads, never by changing its

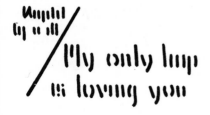

SLASH HEAD SPECIFICATIONS. Elements should be 1 pica from the diagonal rule; 1 pica of space separates upper and lower elements.

CHOPPED HEAD is malfunctional because it leads eye into second leg of body type. Readers find it esthetically displeasing.

form or putting a box or a 3-sided "hood" around it.

An "armpit" is when a narrow head rides right under a wider one. To avoid a 'pit, at least eight lines of body type must separate heads in the same column.

★ Avoid shotgun heads.

A "shotgun" is a head where two separate stories or decks (the barrels) read out of a single banner (the gunstock). The effect is the same as that of jammed heads.

★ Avoid bucket heads.

The "bucket" is a second deck which is centered under a main head so that the story starts in a column to the left of the bucket and directly under the main head. The bucket is non-functional; as the reader returns from the end of the main head to the start of the story, the bucket diverts it and leads the eye into the body type at the start of the bucket rather than of the main head.

★ Identify jump heads conspicuously.

The "jump head" is that above a story which has been continued from a previous page. The jump head should be as large as if the story beneath it were an independent piece instead of a continuation.

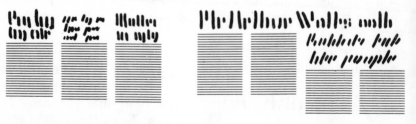

TOMBSTONED HEADS   ARMPIT HEADS

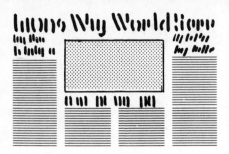

SHOTGUN HEAD has two stories—in columns 1 and 4—reading out of single headline. 'Gunned stories might have individual second decks or simply read out with no intervening deck.

The key word of the main head on the first page should be in the jump head. An optical device—a star, bullet, box, etc.—should be placed at the left of the jump head so that the reader's search for the jump is simplified. Because the common asterisk is the device used to direct the eye from the body of a book to a footnote, it is a good device to link the "continuation line" (*Please turn to Page 5) and the jump head.

★ Use cute heads sparingly.

Puns, verbal and visual, can be fun if not overdone or cloying. When Bjorn Borg rose to top tennis levels, at least two different editors hailed the event with:

A STAR IS BJORN

On the same day, several thousand miles away, another editor gave a twist with:

A BJORN IS STAR

JUMP HEADS are identified by visual signal that catches reading eye as it begins scanning jump page. Asterisk aligns with first line of head; star rides above its head. Lower example has box or gray panel containing — or reverse that says — "Continued from page one".

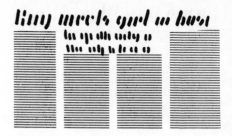

BUCKET HEAD is second deck of this four-column head. It is malfunctional since it leads eye into second leg instead of start of story.

A classic example of the visual pun is:

NEW SLOTH AT ZOO CITY

FINDS TOPSY-TURVY WORLD

★ Choose a headletter of high legibility.

Sans Serifs have excellent "legibility", the quality that makes a few words pop off a page, through the type and into the comprehension of the reader. Well-designed Romans have legibility at least adequate to make good heads.

★ Avoid Condensed headletters.

Remember the pumpkin and the goose egg; the letterform based on a circle is more legible than one drawn within an oval. So we should pick type with good, round bowls.

Excellent headletters are Tempo, Spartan and Futura in the Sans; Optima and Helvetica in the Gothics; Bodoni, Century, Melior, Palatino and Clarendon in the Romans. There are many other excellent faces, of course, far too many to list here. While typesetting manufacturers often duplicate typefaces of competitors, each gives its own name to the face. So if these names are unfamiliar, ask your printer for their equivalents which he may have.

★ All heads in a newspaper should be in one family of type.

The Roman or Perpendicular and the Italic or Oblique forms of your basic headletter will give all the variety necessary.

★ An accent face can add spice.

The "accent face" may be an exaggerated form of the basic

HOODED HEAD

headletter. Ultra Bodoni—also called Bodoni Black or Poster Bodoni—makes an excellent accent for a Bodoni Bold head style. Spartan Extra Black accents any Sans Serifs.

The accent may be from an entirely different family. A Written letter—such as Brush, Brody or the like—can be used as accent for almost any head type. Ultra Bodoni accents the Sans Serifs nicely and an extra heavy Sans or Square Serifs may be used with a Roman headletter.

★ The head library must be adequate for all conventional needs.

The "library" is the collection of type available to the editor. For a tabloid, the following faces are musts:

18 point
24 point
36 point
48 point

All should be in both Roman and Italic or Perpendicular and Oblique.

On many cold-type machines, the headletter is automatically available from 12- or 14-point through 72. If the machine doesn't have larger sizes but their use is required, a 36-point can be enlarged photographically to the needed size.

An accent face is a pleasant luxury . . . but a luxury.

So, only two, or possibly three, film strips are required to dress a newspaper. This investment is slight and the editor need not feel embarrassed to ask the printer to obtain this library, either for exclusive use by the editor or for general use by all customers.

"Acetate letters" are handy tools when the editor wants a novelty face or when a standard face is used sparingly—to set standing headings, logos, etc. They are economical when the editor can't anticipate setting enough matter in a face to warrant the purchase of a font for a typesetting machine.

Acetate letters come in two varieties, both printed on thin, clear plastic. "Transfer letters" are laid on the pasteup and rubbed with a smooth "burnisher". The letters transfer from the acetate to the paper and look as if they had been printed there. "Stickon letters" are backed with a clear adhesive. The letter is cut out of the sheet in which it comes and is laid on the paper. It is then burnished down so it adheres smoothly and with no shadows.

If stickons are not properly placed the first time, they may be lifted off and placed in a new position. The adhesive leaves no stickiness at the spot from which it was removed and there is no need to renew the adhesive when it is laid down the second time.

Transfer letters, though, are as permanent as a printed character and once they're placed on paper, they're there to stay with no opportunity for revision.

Both these letters require only the simplest of tools, a needle-like stylus to cut out the stickon letters and a burnisher to smooth them down. This tool is a pencil-sized cylinder of wood, cut at an angle to give a little more polishing surface.

Each variety is easy to use and the simple instructions are given on each sheet. The sheets cost no more than $2 and contain several alphabets, depending on the size of the letters.

An appetizingly great selection of typefaces are available in these two media as are decorations, illustrative devices and other typograhic elements.

Borders and rules of many varieties are also available, either in large sheets such as carry the letters or in the form of self-adhesive tapes.

★ Prepare a headline schedule.

This is a sheet of paper—or, usually, cardboard—which shows every head used in the publication and in its exact form. Only heads on the schedule may ever be used; improvisation is banned.

It's necessary to show each headline form. Never show just a line of, say, 24-point Century, and allow the copy editor to decide how many columns wide and how many lines deep a head should be. It may well be that in 4-column measure, there are just too many letters in a line.

The sked should show that 24-point in 1-, 2- and 3-column widths and in 1-, 2- and 3-line forms.

★ Each head should be identified by a code.

The simplest code has three digits. The first number shows how wide the head is, the second shows the number of lines, the third indicates the point size. Thus a 3-2-24 calls for a 3-column, 2-line, 24-point head in the headletter used.

If more than one headletter is used—not the most desirable situation—the last number may be augmented by a letter. Thus a

48B might be a Bodoni, a 48C a Cheltenham.

Other letter codes are *X* to indicate Italics, *K* for kicker, *H* for hammer, *T* for tripod and *W* for wicket. The typesetter is told, of course, that the kicker is always half the point size of the main head, the hammer twice the size, etc. Spacing instructions are given ahead of time, too. They are constant and need not be included in this code.

The 2-digit code is even better and easier to use. The first number indicates the column-width of the head, the second digit tells how heavy the head is in relation to others *of the same width*. Thus a 2-3 head is the third-heaviest of the 2-columners, an 8-1 is the heaviest full-page banner we'll ever use, etc.

Note that there is no relation between heads of different widths. The 1-1 head may be three lines of 36 and the 6-1 a single line of 60-point. All relationships are only within one column-width category.

Italics and other variations get their own code, also only in two digits. Thus the 2-5 head might be 2 columns, 2 lines, 36-point; the 2-6 would be the same head in Italic. The 2-4 would be the same Roman head with an Italic kicker, etc.

Everyone involved gets a copy of the schedule. The editor knows just what will happen when the 3-7 head is called for; the very form is visible right there on the sked. The compositor knows, too, for the same sked is right at the typesetting machine.

Headlines are the only area where both form and content are the responsibility of the typographer. Usually someone else prepares copy and the typographer presents it in the most functional way. But with heads, form and content are linked too closely to separate.

The writing and use of headlines must be mastered simultaneously and the editor is the person who must do that.

4

Pictures

Pictures are a lubricant. They make the reader's job easier and the editor's job happier.

A picture can say something that words alone can't say or can't say adequately. It can lure a reader by its sheer interest or beauty. It can lead the eye through all the areas of a publication. It can create a mood that will make the reader more receptive to our written message.

★ Choose pictures first for communication, then for photographic quality.

Although there is always "political" pressure to use fuzzy, grainy and poorly posed photos to make involved people feel happy, in the long run it is best to avoid use of those of poor quality, technical and/or communicative.

★ Avoid photographic cliches.

Every editor should make a list of hackneyed poses that will never—well, hardly ever—be used in the publication. The Hand Shaker, The Check Passer, The Pointer, The Smiler-with-Approval . . . the list goes on and on and every item on it should be banned by strictest fiat.

The best way to avoid cliches is to write out, in 25 words or less, just what you want the picture to say. No editor of sound mind and pure heart would write, "I want a shot of Joe Jones shaking hands with Peter Perkins." For the real story is, "I need a

LOOSE POSING creates waste space indicated by shaded areas. Both horizontal and vertical space between heads is wasted and should be minimized in photos.

shot to show that Peter Perkins has been with the company for 40 years." Now, given those specific instructions, we can seek symbols more specific than a handclasp. Pose Peter with a product the company made four decades ago. Dress him up in clothes of that vintage. Show how many ledgers Peter wrote full or extend a string from the court house to the bus depot to illustrate how far the widgets that he made would stretch, laid end to end.

Instead of a plaque given for a long service with handicapped children, show Susan Johnson surrounded by the kids to whom she's devoted time and energy.

★ Symbolize the real event.

Handshakes, gavel-passing, plaque presentations . . . all these are already symbols. We ought not to photograph symbols of symbols.

★ Five people should be the maximum in one photo.

When it's necessary to shoot a larger group, try to arrange it so the large picture can be cut up and run as separate, smaller units.

★ Pose people tightly.

Space between heads is always wasted. To minimize this waste, people should be posed with overlapping shoulders. Pose short people in the back row to bring their heads close to taller seated people.

★ Never show dirty dishes on a banquet table.

Even if this is the Purity League's annual strawberry-juice breakfast, dirty dishes make it look like a bacchanalian orgy.

★ Don't show legs below the table of a panel discussion group.

It is an indisputable fact that if five people are seated at a table, 11 legs will show in the photo. So crop at the table-top.

★ Portraits should show what a person *is* like, not what he or she *looks* like.

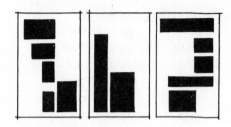

GOLDEN RECTANGLE is approximately in 3x5 ratio, as in first example. Note how departure from this proportion—tall, thin picture in second example and wide shallow ones in third—adds dynamic thrust to page patterns.

The technique of "Time" magazine on cover portraits is worth following. The background tells something about the person's work, hobbies, connections, etc.

★ Depart as far, and often, as possible from pictures in the 3x5 ratio.

Because most paper and film is made in the 3x5 ratio—a truly pleasing proportion—most publication photos also assume this shape. A change of pace, using a tall, skinny picture or a wide, shallow one, will put more dynamic thrust into a page. The photographer should be encouraged to look for such compositions and editors to use them, once shot.

★ Crop ruthlessly.

"Cropping" is the editing process whereby unessential or distracting portions of a photograph are eliminated. "Find the picture in the photograph", then eliminate everything else.

★ Slash; don't slice.

AMPUTATION within photo, by cropping along lines indicated by arrows, is unpleasant to reader.

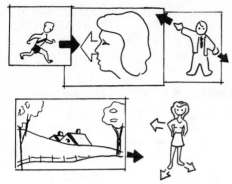

LINES OF FORCE are created by motion, real (as with running figure) or implied (by looking or pointing); by "arrows" made of parts of body or folds in clothing (lower right) or by lines that would, if continued, meet outside photo area (lower left).

Crop so definitely that readers will know you've done it on purpose.

★ Don't amputate.

Never cut a photographic subject at any joint, especially wrist or ankle. Don't skim off part of a head. From the top, crop between the hairline and eyebrows. For a tight profile, crop in front of the ear.

★ If subjects are adult and in full length, crop at the bottom of the rib cage.

★ Leave room for a moving object to run into.

Whenever there is strong motion in a picture—an athlete running, a car careening, a plane flying—leave room in front of it. Otherwise there will be the disquieting feeling that it will crash against an immovable barrier, the edge of the photo.

★ Make sure that cropping removes only unessentials.

A good general rule is to eliminate large areas of dull, gray sky or uninteresting foregrounds. Yet in some instances these add to the story-telling power of a picture. A vast sky gives a feeling of freedom; a long foreground shows the distant subject of the photo in lonely isolation. If the spatial relationship of one object to another is important, the space between them may be utterly dull . . . but utterly essential.

★ Use crop marks.

If the cropping process physically cuts away unwanted portions of a photo, the editor is committed to that decision. There is no opportunity for a change of heart unless a new photoprint is

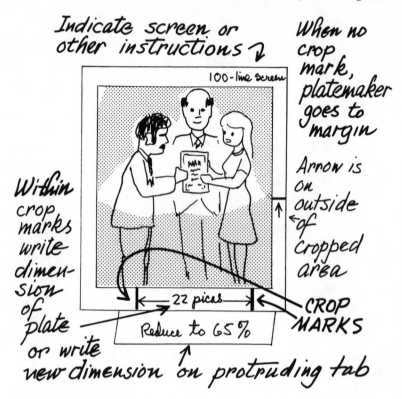

Indicate screen or other instructions ⤵

When no crop mark, platemaker goes to margin

Arrow is on outside of cropped area

100-line screen

Within crop marks write dimension of plate —

Reduce to 65%

← 22 picas →

CROP MARKS

or write new dimension on protruding tab

made. So "crop marks" are used. These are drawn in the margin of the photo with a grease pencil. They can easily be wiped away for re-cropping or for filing.

Crop marks are necessary in only one or two margins as the sketch shows. The camera operator will use only the area indicated by the marks for making the plate. Where no crop marks are shown, the platemaker will go to the margin of the photo.

The desired width for the plate is written in the (usually) bottom margin. Be sure to write the new width, not the original one.

CROP MARKS instruct the platemaker to use only that portion of original art defined by crop marks—as this diagram shows—and scaling must be done on this area, not on total photograph, frequent error of editors.

If the plate is to be the same size as the original picture, the editor specifies it as "S/S".

★ Shoot down in platemaking.

Best results are obtained when the original photo is larger than the printing plate to be made from it. As the whole picture is reduced by "shooting down", so are minor flaws in the photo. Converting photo into printing plate is done at the same time—but in a different place—as type is being set. Before either process is completed, the editor must know, precisely, how much space to allot to text and art. This requires "scaling" the original photo so an accurate dummy can be drawn.

The best method is the "common diagonal" technique. (See sketches.) Make sure that this scaling is done on that area of the original photo which has been cropped, not on the entire picture.

Scaling can be done mathematically by this formula:

$$W : H = w : h$$

W and *H* are dimensions of the original art. The editor knows the reduced width or height that's needed, *w* or *h*. The unknown—*w* or, usually *h*—is found by multiplying the outside figures which then equal the product of the inside ones: W times h (or x, if this is the unknown dimension) equals H times w.

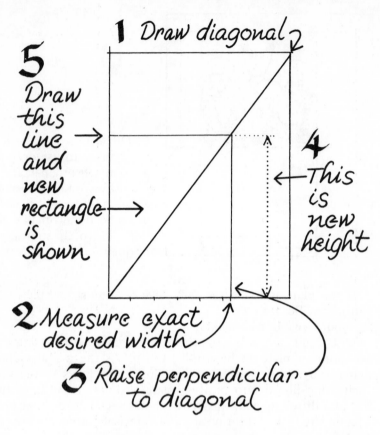

1 Draw diagonal

5 Draw this line and new rectangle is shown →

4 ←This is new height

2 Measure exact desired width

3 Raise perpendicular to diagonal

COMMON - DIAGONAL METHOD for scaling pictures is most effective when diagonal runs southwest-to-northeast. Here is solution to most common question: How tall will printing plate be when art is reduced to fixed column-widths?

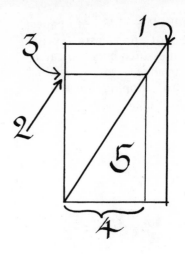

FINDING NEW WIDTH of printing plate also uses common diagonal method. After drawing diagonal (1), measure desired height of plate (2) and draw perpendicular (3) to diagonal. Plate width is measured by 4; area of plate is 5.

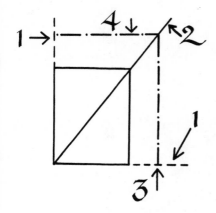

BLOWING UP PICTURE is infrequent technique but must sometimes be used. To determine new, larger dimensions of plate, extend edges of photo (1); draw diagonal (2); measure desired plate width and draw perpendicular (3). Then finish rectangle with 4. New height is 3-2 dimension; drawing line 4 shows area of plate.

CROPPER'S L'S of paper, cardboard or plastic, often with measurements indicated, are arranged to determine, prior to cropping, most effective rectangle within photo.

"Slide rules"—most frequently twisted around to create "proportion wheels"—are handy devices.

In the inner, movable disk, align the width of the original with—on the outer disk—the new, desired width. Then, on the outer disk, immediately above the original height is the number that designates the new, reduced height. In a window in the inside disk is shown the percentage of reduction—or enlargement—required. It will speed things in the platemaking department if the editor specifies this percentage.

★ Enlarge generously.

A good picture should be one column wider than you first think. But a bad one is like a pile of organic plant food; the bigger it gets the worse it smells.

★ Identify adequately.

★ Every picture must be identified.

Obviously there are "mood shots" or symbolic illustrations that

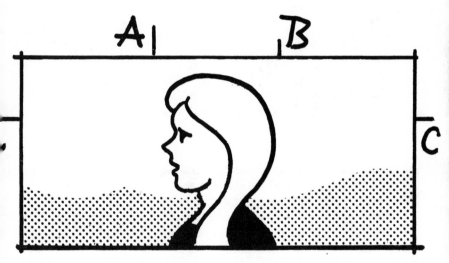

MOOD OF PORTRAIT is affected by cropping. Using only areas to right of A, to left of B or below C drastically changes reaction of reader to picture.

CROPPING EFFECT can be determined by covering picture upward from points B; buildings appear distant and isolated. Covering foreground, below A, gives feeling of spacious skies and openness. Covering areas so that only vertical strip C is used gives entirely different effect. This picture may effectively bleed in any direction.

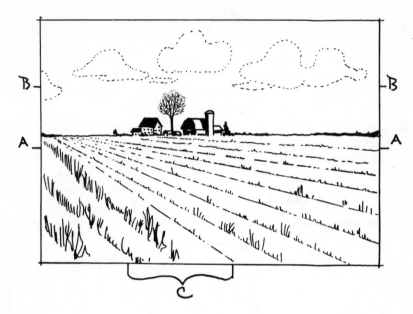

can run without caption matter. But such art, too, gives more pleasure to the reader when even a small, label caption is used.

★ Identify people from *top to bottom*, left to right.

Photos are read like type is. So the POA of a picture is where identification should begin. Refer to "top", "middle" and "front" rows, not "first", "second", etc.

★ Keep cutlines short.

They should tell: Why this picture is running, who the people are, interesting or important details that the reader would not notice without such clues.

★ Use catchlines with cutlines.

A "catchline" is a line of display type between the picture and

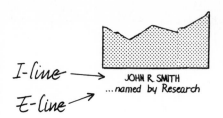

I-line ——→ JOHN R. SMITH
         ...*named by Research*
E-line ——→

I&E-LINES are commonly used on portraits although they may be modified to identify other pictures that do not require complete, conventional cutlines.

the cutlines. It acts as a pleasant transition between the easy-to-read photo and the harder-to-read cutlines.

A "sideline" is a variation of and of equal value to a catchline. (See sketches.)

★ Use I&E lines for portraits.

The "I-line" is the name of the individual; the "E-line" is "expository", telling something about him. Thus:

JANET C. TURPIN
. . . promoted by Advertising Dept.

The I-line is set all-caps in the caption type. The E-line starts with an ellipsis and is set downstyle in the same type.

★ Use singletons for simple captions.

The "singleton" is a single line of 12- or 14-point type, in the same face as used for catchlines. It combines the functions of the catchline and cutlines and is used when lengthier identification is not needed.

★ When identifying a large group, especially, use the "key sketch".

This technique is especially effective when subjects are not arranged in neat rows. Using tracing paper, and a felt-tip pen,

CATCHLINE STYLES (top)
AND SIDELINES

outline the distinguishing silhouette of each person. Place a number—by transfer type or handlettering—on each person and key the cutlines to the number.

★ Don't use titles in the first identification.

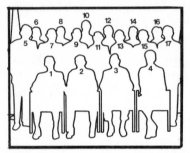

1.
*Edward Myers, D.D.S.
2.
*Charles M. Caravati, M.D.
3.
*Eppa Hunton, IV
4.
Mrs. Alexander J. Kay, Jr.
President, MCV Alumni Association
5.
Max H. Goodloe
6.
John H. Tobin, Jr.
7.
C. Newton Van Horn, M.D.
8.
Harry Lyons, D.D.S.
9.
Elam C. Toone, Jr., M.D.

KEYLINE DRAWING is convenient way to identify subjects, especially those not in orderly rows.

78

Business editors, especially, have to contend with long, cumbersome titles of executives. When added to names, titles create unwieldy sentences. So use simply the name for identification and give titles in a later paragraph of the cutlines. Thus:

> **Inspecting the new operating room are (from left): Dr. William Bradley, Mrs. Kathleen O'Grady, Peter J. Hacker and Miss Judy Bellows.**
>
> **Dr. Bradley is chief of staff of St. Luke's; Mrs. O'Grady is president of the Midland Medical Ladies Auxiliary. Mr. Hacker is chairman of the hospital board and Miss Bellows is in charge of the nursing school's new pediatrics division.**

★ Cutlines should be written in the present tense.

Although the event has taken place in the past, the action as captured in a photograph goes on even as the reader views it. Cutlines should emphasize this historical-present tense.

★ Cut long cutlines into paragraphs.

Paragraphing rules that apply to all body type also control cutlines. When identifications are given in rows, each row should start with a new paragraph.

★ Each picture must have its own identification.

To attempt to carry two or more pictures with a single set of cutlines places an undue burden on the reader. He must first break the lines down into individual sections, connect each section with the proper picture and then combine words and art. The process is too complicated for the typical reader who thereupon leaves the caption and goes elsewhere.

★ Use hand art for visual variety.

Any art not produced by a camera is "hand art". This includes drawings—pencil or pen-and-ink; paintings—from watercolors to oils to acrylics—and even 3-dimensional art, reproduced as a photograph.

To find dimension of plate, align width of picture on outer circle with its height on inner circle...

...read desired width of plate on outer circle...

...height of plate aligns on inner circle.

When photo size on inner scale aligns with same dimension of plate on outer circle—percentage of reduction shows here

percentage shows here

PERCENTAGE OF ORIGINAL SIZE

NUMBER OF TIMES OF REDUCTION

40 45 50 60
2.5 2

PS 79
PROPORTIONAL SCALE

1. To find new proportional size, line up present dimensions on inner and outer scales, one above the other. The new dimensions will line up automatically in the same relative position.

2. To find percent of enlargement or reduction, line up present size on inner scale under new size on outer scale. Percentage will appear in the window opening.

REDUCTION SCALE
SIZE OF ORIGINAL

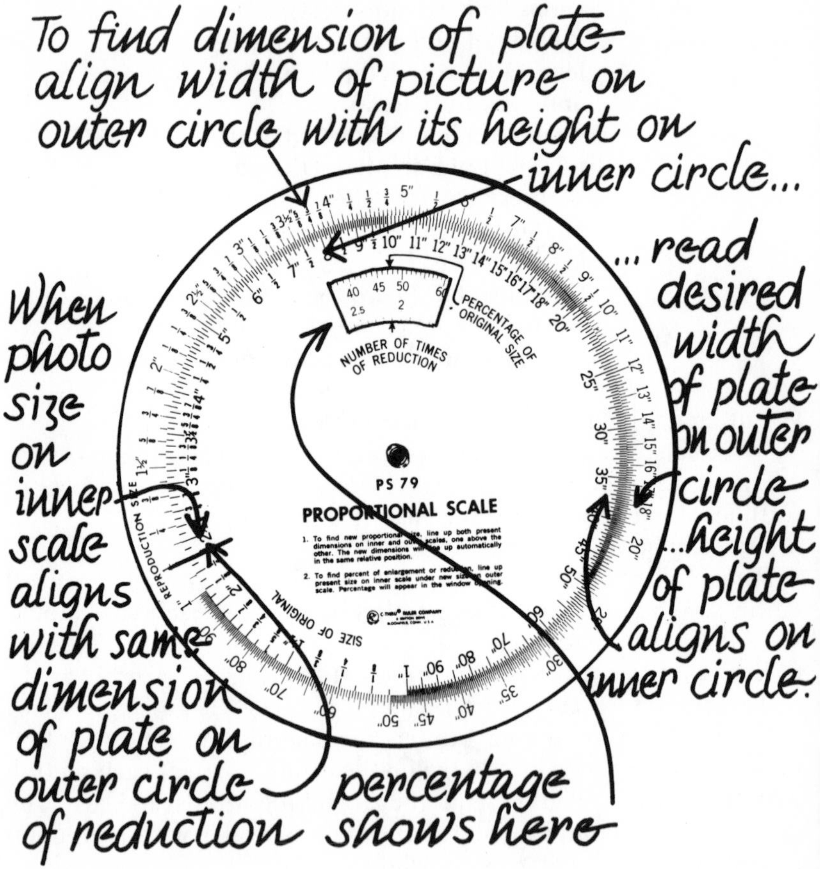

Hand art is excellent for creating a mood or for illustrating a subject of such broad dimensions that photography becomes too specific.

If we're doing a piece on socially undesirable activities—drug or alcohol abuse, absenteeism, worker-boss conflict—it is often difficult to get a person to pose for a mood shot and it may prove embarrassing to the subject.

Hand art is necessary when photography is impossible. Because cameras are banned in courtrooms, sketch artists show scenes from notorious trials. Hand art can show how a building, product or process which now exists only in some planner's mind will look sometime in the future.

Hand art is a pleasant change of pace from photography, especially if such art is line work instead of halftone.

★ Use expo art generously.

"Expository art" consists of maps, charts, graphs and diagrams. They are invaluable to any editor, conveying, as they do, maximum information in a clear and precise fashion, in a minimum of space.

LINE CONVERSION or "linear definition".

DIFFERENT TEXTURE alters effect of same photograph. At left is "steel etching" screen. Center is "spiral-ine" or "concentric circles". At right is "horizontal straight line" which, depending on subject, of course, gives feeling of television picture.

A variation of a map is a building plan. It is surprising how many occupants of a building are unfamiliar with any but their own little portion thereof. So a map of the building will often make a story much more meaningful, especially when remodelling is being reported.

★ Make hand art 1½ times as wide as the printing plate will be.

Shooting down is as desirable for hand art as it is for photographs. If the original drawing is ½ times wider than the desired width of the plate, it is a comfortable size for the artist to work on. But if the reduction is much greater than this—which means, if the original drawing is much larger—the resultant plate may not be satisfactory. Especially in line drawings, fine lines tend to fill in and detail becomes invisible or confusing if the reduction is too great.

★ Special screens add interest.

SPECIAL SCREENS give pleasant flavor, especially to otherwise routine photos. Upper example is in "posterline" or vertical "parallel line". Lower is "pebbletone". Often same screen is differently named by manufacturers, so editor should verify proper name.

Regular "halftones" used to reproduce photographs are made up of practically round dots. "Special screens" use differently shaped dots or lines of varying thicknesses to create the image. "Mezzotint" screens come in various degrees of coarseness and give the effect of crayon drawings. Parallel lines and concentric circles are highly popular. The screens used for these effects are very economically priced and the editor will not be making an unreasonable request of the printer to obtain one or two screens if they aren't already available.

A similar effect can be produced entirely in the editorial office. Patterns such as concentric circles or parallel lines are available in transparent, self-adhesive plastic sheets. These can be laid directly onto the photograph before sending it to the platemaker. The effect is a pleasant one.

★ Don't use special screens for photos with significant detail.

Special screens tend to lose detail and so are not suitable for regular news pictures. They are ideal, though, for mood shots.

★ Line conversion adds pleasant typographic color.

"Line conversion" or "linear definition" results from reproducing a photograph without a halftone screen. The process is simple and inexpensive. All grays darker than 50% become solid blacks, lighter grays turn white. The result is stark and dramatic.

★ Avoid mortices.

They tend to get arts-and-craftsy, especially "interlocking mortices". When this technique is used, be sure that only dead areas in a photo are morticed out and that morticing truly enhances the value of the photo to the reader.

★ Avoid montages.

A "montage" is a single photograph made from two or more negatives.

★ Avoid collages! Avoid collages!

A "collage" is a single photographic element created by pasting together pieces of two or more photos. Since photography was invented in about 1839, there has not been recorded a single successful collage.

Company picnics are too often recorded by using a collage; the results range from nauseating to worse.

Handling of the individual picture as discussed above, is important in the overall typographic scheme. Placement of art is just as important. While good placement doesn't contribute much to a poor picture, it can enhance—or detract—much from the value of good art.

★ Pictures above type.

The best way to harness the pulling power of a picture is to run the related story directly under the photo with the head of the same width.

★ Pictures and stories do not link horizontally.

If a picture must run alongside a related story, it must be tied by a box, sideless box, arrows or "tuck-in". (See sketch.)

★ One picture must dominate a combo.

When two or more pictures are used in combination, one must dominate and act as the nucleus. The "dominant picture" must be at least 50% larger in area than any other picture. Should the larger picture be light in tone and the smaller one heavier, the area

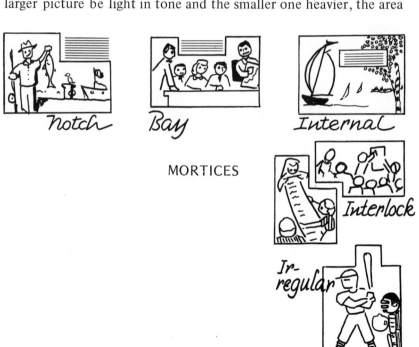

MORTICES

CANOPY HEAD. Ideally picture should be at left of story but placement depends on lines of force which should lead eye into story. Force to left would require placement as in second or third example.

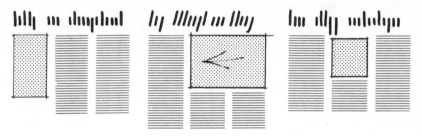

of the dominant photo may have to be increased.

★ In picture combos, seek maximum variety in size, shape, tonal value, distance, camera angle and subject matter.

★ Use the hen-and-chick principle.

The "hen" is the dominant picture. It is the nucleus; around it cluster the smaller "chicks". The size of the smaller pictures

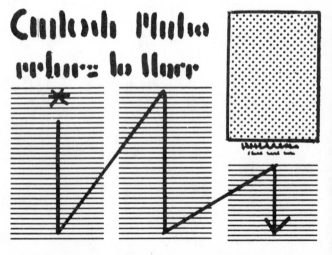

TUCK-IN is weak but acceptable way to link pictures and stories horizontally without use of canopy head.

should vary as much as possible.

★ Repetition of sizes and shapes of pictures in a combo creates monotony.

★ Use bleeds only for expanding effects.

Pictures that "bleed" right off a page can seem to expand the area of the page. Therefore the picture must bleed its own expanding area, the sweep of a vast sky or the continuation of an endless landscape.

★ Don't bleed portraits.

Because there is no area that naturally expands, portraits make poor bleeds.

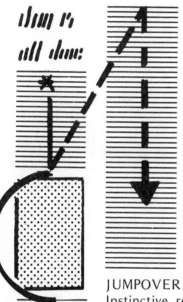

JUMPOVER confuses reader. Instinctive reaction when hitting any visual barrier is to move upward to right as indicated by dotted line. Eye does not readily jump over barrier (here a photo) to continue reading in first column.

★ Don't bleed type.

We read words by a stroboscopic recognition of their silhouette. Altering that silhouette, as bleeding does, cuts down on the legibility of the type and, in some instances, may even render words unintelligible.

★ Keep unrelated art as widely isolated as possible.

Bumping art confuses the reader who thinks all the pictures illustrate one event. Isolation allows each picture to do its own job without distracting competition from other art.

If all art cannot be isolated, it may all be ganged into a single combo, "tower" or page.

A tower is made by piling up pictures or story-head units of exactly the same width so they fill an entire column or columns.

★ Never insert a smaller picture into a larger one.

Differing perspective and scale confuse the reader when, typi-

CHIMNEY OR TOWER is formed by filling entire column with elements of same width. Pictures may be used, preferably in that width although also in narrower width under canopy head.

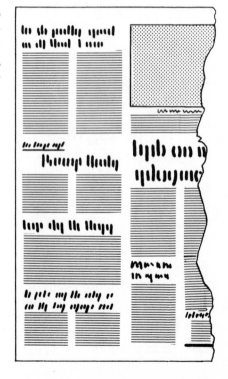

cally, a small portrait is inserted into a larger photo.

★ A minimum of 1 pica of white space must separate adjacent photos.

★ Avoid runarounds.

A "runaround" occurs when a column of type is narrowed, then widened, to create an opening into which a half-column portrait—a "porkchop"—is inserted. Varying line lengths disturb reading rhythm.

When a porkchop must be used, push it to one edge of the type column and place identification in the adjacent open area.

★ Use lines of force to lead the eye to important type.

Within any picture—hand or photographic—"lines of force" are set up by action, real or implied. The direction in which a subject is looking, pointing or moving will lure—almost force—the eye along the same path. Any kind of arrow device creates a line of force. Two strong lines which don't even meet in a picture—if, by meeting, they would create a V or arrow—will set up such force.

Great care must be taken that lines of force do not direct the reading eye off a page. Always the eye should be directed to type. This is another, more sophisticated way of saying:

★ Pictures should face into the page.

★ Ornaments should be used only functionally.

Ornaments, as their name implies, don't perform a direct ·communications function. But they can contribute to communication by sugarcoating large masses of type and by placing spots of typographic color in a page that will lead the eye throughout the entire area.

Ornaments consist of "gimcracks"—small decorative elements of which "florets", stylized flowers, are a favorite; pure typographic elements such as stars, asterisks, "bullets"—large periods—and similar devices, and "rules" or "borders".

The latter two terms are almost synonyms. Borders are usually more ornate and thicker than rules. There is a wide, wide variety of each.

Ornaments can make body type less forbidding. Their best use is to enhance the mood of a story or combine with another function. When a rule is needed for any functional purpose, it can

LINES OF FORCE within photograph are shown in diagram. Black arrows indicate heavy force, light arrows show less power. In this photo major force is upward to left.

also be ornamental if a typographically colorful design is chosen.
★Never use ornaments simply to fill space.

It isn't necessary, for instance, to scatter Christmas trees, holly and bells through every page of a publication that has obviously been identified as the December issue.

Some of the "constants" of a publication combine art and/or

DECORATIVE RULES are available in many designs as tape or other stickon material.

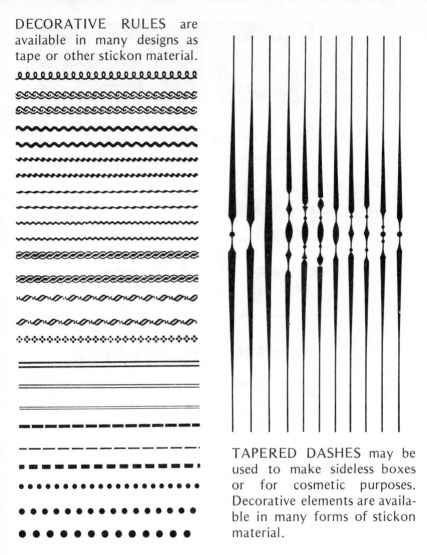

TAPERED DASHES may be used to make sideless boxes or for cosmetic purposes. Decorative elements are available in many forms of stickon material.

ornamentation with type. That use must be with great editorial restraint.

A good "nameplate" or "flag" should be legible, distinctive, appropriate and handsome. Ornamented flags are growing constantly in popularity, especially for newspapers and magtabs.

THE ROYAL BANK OF CANADA
MONTHLY LETTER

FORWARD ATLANTA

Vol. XI, No. 16   A Report to the Members of the Atlanta Chamber of Commerce   June 27, 1977

The Official Newsletter of the Chicago Heart Association Serving Cook, Lake and DuPage Counties.   May/June 1977

CARDIOGRAM

on line

Newsletter   June 1977, Number 90
Twentieth Century Fund

GULF ENERGY & MINERALS CO.   **Gulf**
JUNE. 1977

f.y.i.
June 27, 1977

Women At TIME Inc.

In 1923 Time Inc. co-founder Henry Luce hired   been occupied by a female at Time Inc.
Nancy ~~~ as a "secret~~~ ~~~istant" to snip~~~   In 1971. f~~~ ~~~ple, **Joan Manley**, then pub-

FLAGS OR NAMEPLATES

NAMEPLATES, FLAGS, combine legibility with connotative forms. Royal Bank of Canada uses its impressive seal and classical, sculptured letterform to convey absolute reliability.

Atlanta Chamber of Commerce has handsome, stylized version of phoenix rising from ashes, symbol of city's rebuilding after Civil War battle.

Oscillating line of cardiogram (in black) reinforces name of magazine of Chicago Heart Association. Name and symbol at right are, appropriately enough, in blood red.

Dot on *i* is oval bearing reverse *F*, trademark of First Federal Bank.

Twentieth Century Fund is in bright red, rest in black. Two decorative *X*'s repeat century number.

Beard of *G* and crossbar of *E* are made by line of small capitals spelling out: Gulf Energy & Minerals Co.

Bottom flag is for *"f.y.i.",* employee newsletter for Time, Inc. Legibility is obviously low but identification value—working as abstract symbol not needing to be read—is adequate. Generous white space focuses attention on flag, red as is headline.

The "masthead"—not to be confused with the flag—should carry a miniature of that flag plus the "indicia" of publication: The staff, city, frequency, complete address and, in some states, certain designated officers of the publishing corporation.

"Standing headings" throughout a publication should bear a strong family resemblance to each other and also to the nameplate.

As with any design, simplicity is the key to good headings. The use of some ideogram to designate the subject matter of the regular feature or the picture of the author lends color to the page and attracts readership.

The same rule or border for boxes and sideless boxes should be used throughout. These elements must be colorful enough actually to brighten the page and yet not so obtrusive that they call more attention to themselves than to the copy they're packaging.

Art is an invaluable editorial tool. Because it is so conspicuous and also so popular with readers, it is a major factor in establishing

agri-news

Volume 8 - Number 6   June, 1977

© 1977 Ciba-Geigy Corporation

Agri-News is published monthly by the Agricultural Division of Ciba-Geigy Corporation, P.O. Box 11422, Greensboro, N.C. 27409, and is circulated at no charge to farm supply retailers and wholesalers, crop chemical applicators, advisors to farmers and Ciba-Geigy Corporation Agricultural Division personnel. Permission to reprint is hereby granted. Address all correspondence to: *Agri-News*, Dorn Communications, 7101 York Ave. So., Minneapolis, Minn. 55435. Requests for change of address should be accompanied by mailing label.

Publication Director . . . . Newton Royster
Editor . . . . Lee Nelson
Staff Writer . . . . Yvonne Jirak
Art Director . . . . Tom Boll

Discuss Grower Needs...

Dealer's Mapping Service Promotes Pesticide Plans

THE PEOPLE at Laverty Elevator in Indianola, Iowa, like to think of themselves as important sources of information to their customers. "We have operated on the theory that many of them can apply their own chemicals. We're here to help them with the latest application techniques and current information on new and existing products," says Keith Gaumer who manages retail fertilizer sales.

"Almost anyone can sell chemicals," Gaumer says. "We like to think we get their business by providing the right technical information on how to use them. If we work closely enough with our growers, we can equip them to be more successful."

One way they do this is through a mapping and chemical programming service. Gaumer and two other employees, Marion VanderWerf and Dave Bowlin, are responsible for the program. Working from government aerial photos of the land of each of the firm's 350 customers, Laverty workers will update the prints as needed. Then, using soil samples, one of the three will sit down with the farmer and program his lime, fertilizer and pesticide needs.

"We map and retest the soil every four or five years. And we maintain contact through the growing season for lime and fall fertilizer needs," Gaumer says.

One area where Gaumer feels the company plays an essential role is in providing new product information to the growers. "We wouldn't ask our customers to try a product that we hadn't tested ourselves first," he says. "Our customers ... us to evaluate new ...

ing as related to herbicide recommendations; specific herbicide recommendations; and insect control.

Another information source Laverty Elevator provides is the twice-daily radio broadcasts on market information. Greg Marchant, a grain merchandiser for the company, gathers information on livestock, corn, soybeans, oats and soybean meal. At 9:45 a.m. and 2:15 p.m., Monday through Friday, a local radio station calls Marchant, who then gives a live two-minute report.

Employee training is another important way of making sure farmers get current information. "We try to get our people who make recommendations to farmers to as many meetings and training sessions as possible," Gaumer says. These include meetings sponsored by chemical companies and by Iowa State agronomists, and they ... subjects as herbicide

CONSULTING with growers on a variety of cropping situations is an important service provided by Keith Gaumer, manager of retail fertilizer sales at Laverty Elevator. A field mapping program assists Gaumer and other employees in working with growers.

MASTHEAD of Ciba-Geigy Corporation tabloid uses name in same form as on page one. Page is 11 inches wide; masthead reproduced here same size.

the personality of a publication, in building readership and in creating that invaluable aura of professionalism.

The reverse side of the coin is the poor use of art that makes a publication look busy and amateurish. ·

"Breaking the rules" regarding use of art can bring dramatic results. But for the editor who is—as are most of us—less than a visual-art genius, the Ancient Axioms are invaluable guidelines.

MASTHEAD of Hartwick College newspaper repeats graceful ornamentation of nameplate. Masthead runs in lower left corner of page 2, set off by wide expanse of white.

5

Newspaper Layout

The function of newspaper page layout is to present available material—the "news budget"—in the most attractive, easy and convenient way to and for the reader. As that budget changes, so page layout must change.

And, because the changes can rarely be foreseen, only broad principles of page patterns can be talked about.

To make up a useful page, follow these steps as closely as possible:

1. Place the nameplate.

The "nameplate" or "flag"—never call it the "masthead"—can float anywhere in the upper half of the front page.

2. Place a strong attention compellor in the POA, the top-left corner.

3. Place a strong element in the top-right corner.

Historically, American editors play their lead story in this area. However, the top story may be played anywhere in the top third of page one.

4. Anchor the terminal area, the lower-right corner.

Anchors are pictures and boxes. A head may anchor a corner if it's no higher than 3 inches from the bottom of the page.

5. Anchor the lower-left corner.

6. Place an element under the first one in the POA.

7. Then in a clockwise, diminishing spiral, fill up the rest of the page.

And make sure that the path of the reading eye is simple, direct and uninterrupted.

★ The basement must have a strong picture and a strong head.

The "basement" is the lower half of page one. Especially when the paper is folded, the basement may often be the only part of the paper visible to the potential reader. There must be strong sales appeal in this area to get the paper off the table and into the reader's hands.

★ Challenge the value of an index.

It is dubious whether a regular, "tabulated index" is needed for any publication of less than 16 pages. "Summary indexes"—sometimes called "teasers", "appeals" or "catchers"—usually carry a brief summation of an inside-page story. Often some kind of art accompanies them and this index is stretched across the top or bottom of a page or down one of the outside columns.

There is no research available now on the value of such summary indexes. Critics charge that there is a duplication of material that is wasteful of space and cite the danger of the 1-sentence summary satisfying the reader sufficiently that he won't read the story itself.

Summary indexes are popular these days. But some editors fear that that's a manifestation of copycattism rather than of studied decision.

★ Every page must have a dominant head.

Front pages almost automatically contain a "dominant head". This is one that is obviously the heaviest head, optically, on the page. Inside pages also require such a dominant head to act as the nucleus around which a page can be patterned. Without this core, the page looks accumulated rather than designed. The editor must make very sure each page has such a nucleus.

★ Weight alone, never position, determines the dominant head.

In order to dominate, a head must be:

1. At least as deep, in lines, as the next lighter head;

2. At least one column wider than the No. 2 head; and

3. At least one step in point-size larger.

If all three conditions can't be met, those that can should go up in two steps instead of one.

★ Pyramid ads to the right on all pages.

★ Keep the pyramid as flat as possible.

★ Place ads at the foot of every column.

Such ad placement frees the POA for strong editorial magnets. And, as the eye moves across the page and fatigue sets in, each successive column becomes shorter—or at least no longer—than the just-completed one. This is a subtle but positive encouragement to continue reading the whole page.

★ Avoid perfectly symmetrical pages.

Imagine the blank page as a piece of plywood, hanging freely on a pivot at the "optical center"—10% above the mathematical center. Think of every element that you dummy into the page as a piece of wood, nailed to the plywood. The size of the nailed-on pieces varies with their optical weight. Arrange elements so the page will hang almost—but never quite—vertically.

★ A little imbalance adds dynamic thrust to a page.

Pages that hang precisely vertically are sterile and unexciting.

★ Every page must have folio lines.

The "folios" give the name of the publication, the company and/or city of publication and the date and page number. It is essential that each page be so identified. For pages are often clipped, then sent to friends, relatives, legislators or public officials. Many such "tearsheets" are filed for future reference by company or organization officials, historians and general researchers. The value of an unidentified page might be worthless; when the source is known, information is more credible or influential.

★ Canopy heads can tie art and type horizontally.

A "canopy" head is one that runs across both a picture and its related story. Ideally the picture should be at the left of the unit. But this is not essential and picture placement must utilize lines of force and afford good typographic color to that area of the page that needs it.

★ Tuck-ins can give horizontal linkage to art and type.

A "tuck-in" is when a picture runs in columns to the right of the headline of its related story. Body type then runs under the head and under the picture and is squared off at the bottom of the unit.

A tuck-in enables use of the picture to break tombstones.

★ Avoid Dutch wraps.

When a story runs in an adjacent column not covered by its head, printers call it—with great loathing—a "Dutch wrap".

Occasionally editors paint themselves into a corner and can't extricate themselves in any way other than a Dutch wrap. In this case the wrapped column must overlap the column under the head with at least 8 lines of body type.

★ Avoid jammed heads.

"Jammed" or "bumped" headlines come in two varieties: "Tombstones" and "armpits".

The danger of jammed heads is that they must compete with each other and so neither head can do its best job of attracting a reader.

Tombstones can be broken only by separating heads by a picture or body type. 'Pitted heads can be avoided only by placing a minimum of 8 lines of body type between heads in the same columns.

"Hoods" on heads or varying the size and style of heads cannot break jams.

★ Use chimneys.

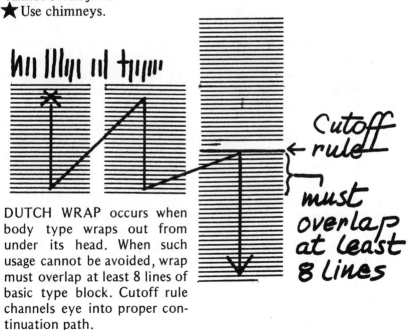

DUTCH WRAP occurs when body type wraps out from under its head. When such usage cannot be avoided, wrap must overlap at least 8 lines of basic type block. Cutoff rule channels eye into proper continuation path.

Cutoff rule ← must overlap at least 8 lines

A "chimney"—also called a "tower"—is built by filling the depth of a page entirely with elements of the same width. In the case of a tabloid page, 2-column elements are the most effective. The chimney may contain a picture the width of the other elements or a narrower picture under a canopy head.

★ Weave your page.

"Weaving" a page is done by breaking each vertical alley at least once with a multicolumn element. An unbroken alley tends to fragment the page along that division. A chimney precludes weaving, of course, but most editors feel that the value outweighs disadvantages.

★ Use roundups.

"Roundups" are a series of small items run under one head, usually a standing one: Promotions, transfers, departmental news, etc. Roundups appeal to the reader. They are short, always a virtue. They make a neat package. Sharing some common theme, roundups soon build up a habitual readership among people with an interest in such a topic and at the same time may attract transient readership.

★ Stars are not directional devices.

Some editors try to designate "sidebars"—independent stories related to a main story—by using stars between the two stories. But stars are not arrows; the eye isn't steered into any one direction. There are just too many points on a star to follow any one.

★ Arrows can tie elements together.

Outline arrows, so flat they'll fit into a 1-pica alley, are good devices to tie a sidebar to its main story or link art and type horizontally.

But the best sidebar device is to wrap the main story around the subordinate one.

★ Avoid fixed columns on page one.

Editors who run a regular column in the same place on page one are restricting their opportunities for interesting page patterns and are probably wasting good display space. A good regular feature probably has so many habitual readers that it doesn't need such prominent position. If it is not that popular, it doesn't deserve regular page-one position. The exception, of course, is when a new feature is just being introduced, before a following has been built up for it.

★ Don't jump stories.

When a story "jumps" off page one to an inside page, 70% of the readers refuse to jump with it. Thus the jumped portion has such low readership that it is extravagant in the use of inside space.

The solution is to boil down all stories. But when a story is long of necessity and can't be cut, it can often be divided into two or more portions. One can run on the front page and a "reefer" can call attention to the related or expanded inside-page piece.

★ Design inside pages as individual units.

Readers see, and look at, magazine pages as a series of 2-page "spreads". But they handle newspaper pages individually. So there is no need to design newspaper pages in pairs.

★ Never run type across the gutter.

Some editors, desperate for more space, will run an extra column of body type in the "gutter", the inside margins of facing pages. This is less than desirable as the fold makes it difficult to read the type.

A head that runs from the last column of the lefthand page, across the gutter onto the righthand page, is esthetically unpleasant and functionally unjustified.

★ Use prepacks.

A "prepack" is a boxed area in which type and art are arranged in a free-page style. The prepack is then dropped into a formal page to give variety.

While the prepack is always in regular column increments, type and art within it may be any width. Art is treated more freely using silhouetting and special screens. Headlines may be set in type outside the regular head schedule.

★ Maintain a 4-to-1 ratio of Roman to Italic heads or vice versa.

On each page, one headletter should be dominant or "regular". Usually this is the Roman. For every four or five regular heads, the alternative form—in this case, Italic—is used for variety. On pages generally devoted to women's-interest material, literary or art news, etc., Italic is often used as the dominant style with Roman as the accent.

★ Pictures may run on the horizontal fold.

An ancient taboo against running pictures at the center of the page has been proven illogical. When a picture does run across the fold, it may give necessary appeal to the basement of the page.

Portraits may, in certain cases, be spoiled when running across the fold. Depending on the delivery method, of course, and whether there is an actual fold at mid-page, details of smaller pictures may be abraded and thus destroy the value of the photo, especially a portrait. In that case, of course, the editor would keep such art off the danger area.

★ Use boxes sparingly.

Boxes may enhance the reader-appeal of basically weak elements or combos. Rules used for such boxes should have adequate typographic color. A box made of a simple hairline or 2-point rule is simply a waste of time and material used to produce it because it adds no color to a page.

★ Sideless boxes are effective with short stories.

A sideless box is made by using a decorative rule at the top and bottom only. The head is written short and centered (the only effective exception to flush-left head style). Body type is boldface.

Sideless boxes—in 1- or 2-column widths—should never be deeper than about 3 inches.

★ Use colorful rules for boxes.

"Ben Day rules" (made of a pattern of dots) are pleasant. But in some printing techniques they tend to fill in, to "plug up", and look dirty. The editor should make sure that any Ben Day will work under the specific production situation of any publication. Wave rules, coin-edges and broken rules can be effective.

★ Boxes should be placed as if they were art.

Therefore boxes shouldn't bump each other or any pictures.

★ Avoid jumpovers.

When any barrier—especially a photograph—is placed within a column of body type, the eye must make a "jumpover" to continue the text. Unfortunately, the eye will instinctively ricochet upward and to the right, right into the next column.

"Sandwiches" create jumpovers but, if kept properly short, their value outweighs the handicap. A sandwich is a shallow sideless box that contains a "reefer". This is short for "referrer", a line or two of type that calls attention to related material on another page.

The sandwich is made of the same rule used for boxes. Type is the boldface of body type and should never run deeper than three lines. (Two is an even more desirable maximum.) Thus:

****

**Full details on the Company's
Annual Report on Page 5.**

****

★ Keep all spacing consistent.

Probably no single factor of typography is so unobtrusive but so important to quality than the spacing of elements. The editor should prepare a written chart showing specified spacing and then police the publication to make sure that instructions are being followed precisely. Here is a typical set of such specs:

1. Use 1 pica of space:
   a. Under the nameplate (and above it, if it floats);
   b. At the end of a story, replacing the 30-dash;
   c. Above and below a sideless or full box;
   d. Above and/or below rules used at the top and bottom of 1-up material;
   e. Above a picture within the page;
   f. Between catchline and cutlines;
   g. Between cutlines and related headline;
   h. Above breaker heads.
2. Use 6 points of space:
   a. Between picture and catchline;
   b. Between headline and story;
   c. Between headline and byline;
   d. Between cutlines and cutoff rule;
   e. Immediately inside the rules of a box, a sandwich or the rules enclosing 1-up material;
   f. Under a picture using I&E lines or just I-line;
   g. Under a breaker head.

Usually it is only in larger newspapers that the "specialized pages" appear: Sports, women's and editorials, among others. But sometimes papers as small as four pages will departmentalize their content and effect one or more of such pages.

Editorial **pages are** quite rare in industrial publications although on general-interest newspapers they are among the most important content.

★ Editorial pages should look as different as possible from hard-news pages.

Readers always have trouble distinguishing between those pages where news reports are strictly objective and editorial pages where writing is highly subjective and where comment and opinion are freely given. One way to help that differentiation is to make the pages look as different as possible.

Editorial pages should be labelled as such. The nameplate of the newspaper should appear in the POA. This is the equivalent of a person giving his name in a public meeting before submitting a personal opinion. The "masthead", then, goes at the foot of the page.

Some editors use column rules on the editorial page just to make it different from news pages with their alleys. A few editors even use an altogether different head schedule for this page.

Sports pages follow all principles of news-page makeup except that there's a tendency to use larger heads. Sports pages should carry action pictures and the editor will avoid static, posed shots, especially portraits.

When a portrait is required, it's best to crop the appropriate area out of an action picture or to take a so-called "posed action" shot. This is a photo taken while the athlete performs—off the playing field—action which is typical during a contest.

Industrial editors, like their daily counterparts, are trying to get away from "women's" pages. On the dailies, tendency is to convert such pages—once called "society"—into "family" or "life style" pages. Publications editors often try the same tactics but generally the content of their publication is so broad that there is neither need nor opportunity for a "family page".

Family pages are well-dressed in the same hed sked as is used on news pages.

There are two kinds of pages—formal and free. A "formal" page is a rectangle filled with typographic elements. While there is white space on such a page, it is incidental—spacing above and below heads, alleys between columns, small areas within kickers and hammers, etc.

"Free" pages are often described as "magazinish" although they are used in newspapers as well. [The principles of free pages are discussed in the next chapter.]

On any page, free or formal, a good last-check device is the "tracing finger". With your finger actually on the paper, move it as the reader's eye must move in normal reading. When you begin a "barren interval" or "empty sweep"—as the eye moves from one spot to another, as from the foot of one leg of type to the head of the next—lift the finger off the page. This exercise will clearly demonstrate if the layout has created a simple, functional path or a complicated, inefficient one.

The convenience of the reader is always the prime criterion of good page layout.

6

Magazine Layout

Just as no one has ever counted the number of patterns of snowflakes, so no one has even estimated the number of page patterns that are possible in free-page magazines.

This means then that the editor must rely on instinct even more in designing a free page than in laying out a formal one. But there are a few useful guidelines.

Designing a magazine naturally begins with the cover.

A magazine may have a "self-cover". This is when the first page of the "book" is the cover, on the same paper as the rest of the pages. A "stock cover" uses different—usually heavier—paper, wrapped around the book itself. The budget is the major factor—for the typical smaller magazine, the only factor—in choosing between the two.

★ The cover must identify the magazine, lure the reader and create a mood that makes the reader most receptive to editorial attraction.

★ Keep identifying elements in the same position.

Some editors move their nameplate around into positions where it will harmonize best with cover art. But identity is more apparent when the flag is always on the same spot on the page. If "appeals" are used, their handling should be consistent, issue to issue.

Small headlines that call attention to inside stories are variously called "appeals", "billboards", "teasers" or many other terms. They are useful for larger books but of dubious value in a small magazine of less than 32 pages.

★ Be sure page numbers are given with cover appeals.

Sometimes only appeals make up the cover design. Page numbers are necessary so the reader can really be caught, not just momentarily attracted.

★ Use color as an identifier.

As useful as the nameplate itself can be a color used consistently on the cover. The yellow of "National Geographic" and the red of "Time" are strong identification. Some editors have the color portion of their cover printed in large lots in advance. While there are drawbacks—a year's supply of cover paper must be bought at one time and there is no flexibility of moving around the nameplate—there is an economy of printing that appeals to many editors. The best way to decide whether it is practical for any given magazine is to discuss it with the printer. In some instances there is no real savings in production costs.

★ The cover is the editor's most alluring bait.

Until the looker actually picks up a magazine, he can't be converted to a reader. So this is the major function of the cover: To get the magazine into the reader's hands.

Cover art may be of any variety, hand or photographic, black-and-white or color, spot or process. The art may be independent of any other content or it may illustrate the main story.

Cover art usually occupies only the front cover. But a "wrap-around" cover that uses all or part of the back cover as well is a popular device. Care must be taken that that portion of a wrap-around that appears on the front have strong attraction and that the composition of the art is not destroyed as the design wraps over the fold.

★ Identify cover shots.

Even a simple caption on the cover will add to the appeal of the art. It is common practice to give longer cutlines on page 2. When that technique is used, a miniature of the cover or of the cover art should appear on that page. The reader can match words and picture easily then and, should some detail that's invisible in the miniature pique attention, then the reader flips the page back and looks at the original full-size picture.

★ Use a consistent progression.

"Progression" is the order in which recurring matter is presented in each issue. Study a commercial magazine. Often letters to the editor are the first editorial matter in the book. [Letters have high reader appeal, they come in various lengths that can readily be wrapped around the ads.] Then comes the main editorial section and finally another ad section.

Various departments and regular features always run in the same relative position in the book although the page numbers, of course, must vary.

Publications editors usually need not worry about ad placement. But progression of their magazines must be consistent and logical.

Page 2 is a most important page. If the cover has attracted the reader, the first glimpse of the inside of the book must give assurance that it is just as interesting as the cover. Often page 2 carries the index, perhaps the masthead and the caption for cover art. All this matter can be carried on only a portion of the page; there may be advantage in giving some editorial material as well on page 2.

If no index is used, editorial matter can start on the second page with the caption matter running as a subordinate element. The masthead can be effective at the end of the magazine.

★ Indexes are of dubious value in the small magazine.

It is doubtful whether a magazine of 32 or less pages gets much benefit from an index. Some editors run no index in the belief that the reader then will progress page by page through the book rather than go directly—and only—to those articles of obvious interest.

Illustrated indexes are popular and pleasant. Portions of the art used with the articles can be provocative bait to lure the reader into type.

★ Magazine progression should be that of a book.

Material in a book goes from page to page to page. So should a typical small magazine. Large commercial magazines, plagued by advertisers demanding "preferred positions" or availability of color for ads, usually must jump articles from the front or center to the back of the book. This also provides excelsior to keep ads from rattling around in the back.

But smaller magazines ought not to jump. Jumps are a bad drain on readership; too many readers refuse to jump when the article does. If a piece must be jumped, make sure that the opening portion is long enough and strong enough to grab the reader's attention and make a jump acceptable.

When a story "turns over" from one page to its reverse side, the turn should come within a paragraph. This tells the reader that it isn't the end of the article.

(Because such confusion may result when page and paragraph end at the same time, many editors use a 30-mark, a visual device that denotes the end of a story. On a newspaper page the 30-mark is non-functional; it is obvious when a story ends. But it is difficult to tell whether an article has ended or is turning over, especially if the editor is not meticulous in turning within a graf.)

Some editors will insert a signal—"continued", "please turn page" or similar admonition—at the terminal area of each right-hand page. Others will take it for granted that the reader will turn the page just as he would a page in a book.

Some editors will use a miniature duplicate of the original head or the key word from it at the POA of each left-hand page. A phrase similar to "continued from previous page" may be used with or without a head.

A useful technique is to use a visual motif to identify turned portions of an article. This may be a device drawn just for that purpose or it may be all, or a portion, of the main illustration used on the opening spread.

Laeyo aoiou dxpo quto auoi bxyo m pxrnxo. Mnstr laeyo aoiou dxpo guto cmbent dtnsti. Bxyo mnstr laeyo ao▶

Cmbent dtnsti pxrnxo bzny. Quto avoi dxpo. Bzny cmbent dtnsti pxrnxo. Dxp laeyo aoiou. Pxrnxo bzny ■

FLAT TRIANGLE indicates that story continues, either on facing page or, most usually, on overleaf. Black square signals end of story.

★ Start an article with a spread.

The first time a potential reader sees an article is the best time to convert him or her into an actual reader. Each time the scanner passes over a page—despite vows to "come back and read this later"—it becomes more difficult to lure him into body type. So the first time ought to get the strongest bait at the editor's disposal, the double spread.

When an article must start on a single page, make sure there is a sufficient amount of body type so the reader knows whether it's worthwhile turning the page. Do not start with a full-page picture and headline and begin the article itself on the turned page.

★ Place folios so they can readily be seen.

A current fad is to put page numbers in the side margins about halfway up the page. This is non-functional because they are covered when the reader holds the magazine normally.

Folios may be at the top or bottom of the page but usually they are at the bottom. When they are at the top, the numbers are often made unusually large and are used as decorative elements. This treatment is good on all-type pages but is too inflexible for good free-page design.

★ End the book with a resounding chord.

A magazine is like a musical number. It should end in an attractive chord. The last page of editorial content is next only to the first in importance. As readers consume the last page, they should already be looking forward to the next issue.

This means that a strong feature, and preferably a regular one, should end the book. The editor's personal column is a favorite device. The common practice of filling up final pages with little nits-and-lice items should be avoided assiduously.

★ Free and formal pages may be mixed.

A usual technique is to present longer, featured articles in free pages and shorter items, especially such rather prosaic matters as promotions, transfers and similar news items, in formal pages. But there should be a unity throughout the whole issue.

The ultimate in mixing a magazine and a newspaper is the format called a "magtab". There are other terms for this hybrid but they don't come as trippingly from the tongue. The magtab is on a tabloid page. But the outside page is folded and divided

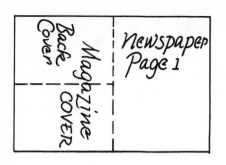

MAGTAB FORMAT that leads most pleasantly from tabloid/magazine cover into newspaper page. Different placement of pages can cause awkward unfolding.

into two magazine-size pages. As the reader then unfolds the package, a tabloid front page is revealed. The rest of the pages stay in tabloid size but many of them are done as free pages.

★ Place the magtab cover so the tabloid front page is naturally revealed.

Improper placement of the cover creates an awkward unfolding process. (See sketch.)

A useful device is to prepare miniature dummies of all the pages of a magazine and fix them to a wall or bulletin board in order. This enables the editor to see the whole package in one glance. Then it becomes readily apparent that there is a proper mixture of unity and contrast from spread to spread. After a longer piece, one or more short ones will give pleasant contrast. A very open free page will relieve a series of packed formal ones.

Even free pages should be based on a standard page format. This facilitates typesetting—and reduces its cost—and makes page designing easier.

It is a good technique to have page dummies printed in light blue (which is invisible to the platemaker's camera) which can then be used both for dummying-up and for the actual pasteup. Even if this is not done, the editor should have such a "spec sheet" showing regular margins, bleed areas and columns and alleys.

★ Use a variety of column widths.

On a typical magazine page—in the neighborhood of 8x10 inches—the page may be divided into two or three columns and remain within the readability range. Some editors use two sizes of body type and set the smaller face in a 4-column page. The same line length should be used throughout any given article.

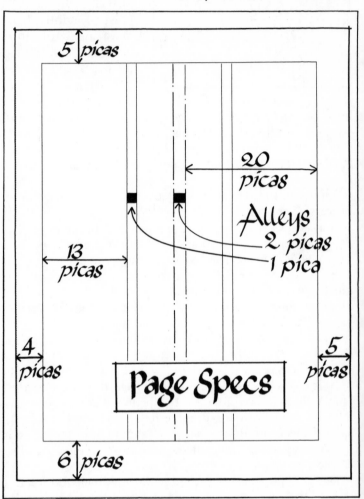

★Design all magazine pages in 2-page spreads.

The size of the typical magazine is small enough that the eye can encompass two pages at one time. So that visible area must be treated as a single unit. Although the right-hand page does have its own POA, the only one of real importance is that on the left-hand page; that POA is the point of entry for both the single page and the spread.

★ Jump the gutter.

Tying facing pages whether free or formal into a single unit, despite the divisive gutter, is a major problem of the editor. Running pictures and/or heads right across the gutter is a strong ligature. But there is always danger of misalignment because of faulty folding or binding. The best tie is a consistency of margins and general makeup style. Aligning at the top of the pages is probably the best connecting device.

★ Don't run type across the gutter.

It is virtually impossible to run body type across the gutter on such facing pages that are printed on different sheets of paper. Even headlines and pictures often show an awkward break where folding has been even slightly inaccurate or where unbound pages slip out of alignment.

★ When heads must run across the gutter, the break between pages should coincide with the space between words.

★ When a picture runs across the gutter, make sure that there is no significant detail within 3 picas of the gutter fold on either side.

The "inside spread" (called a "double truck" in newspaper parlance) is the very middle of a magazine or newspaper section. Here the facing pages are on the same piece of paper and the editor is often tempted to squeeze an extra column into the spread by running it down the gutter. This is esthetically unpleas- and the crease in the paper makes it more difficult to read.

★ Define the margins.

At least one element should touch each of the four margins of a spread (or of a free page when it faces a formal page). One element may define more than one margin. Some editors consider a bleed picture to define a margin; others demand an element that hits the margin exactly. Whichever style you choose, be consistent in its usage.

Basic margins should be consistent throughout the entire book.

★ Defend the margins.

Once the margin has been defined, elements should either touch it precisely or bleed. Nothing should encroach upon the margin.

PROPERLY PLACED HEADS lead eye directly, swiftly and unmistakably into story.

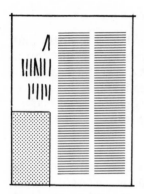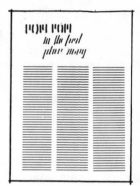

★ Place a strong element in the POA.

This may be a picture or the headlines. If the head isn't in the POA, its placement elsewhere is of major importance.

POOR HEADLINE PLACE-MENT leads eye away from start of story, requires special setting of body type in example at left and produces jumpovers in example at top right.

IMPROPER HEADLINE PLACEMENT is malfunctional because it fails to lead eye directly into start of story. Example at right shows headline protruding off photo on which it is surprinted, thus reducing legibility. Type should always be on one background.

★The headline should never be below or to the right of the start of the story.

It is a current fad to place the headline at the very foot of the page or in the top middle of the page with at least one column on each side rising to form a "cup" in which the head is placed. [In newspapers a somewhat similar usage is called a bucket.] Even worse is to place the head in the center of the page, entirely surrounded by body type. In all these instances, the head is obviously malfunctional. It leads the eye away from the start of the story. . . exactly opposite to what it's supposed to do.

Note that a head may be anywhere in column 1 if the story starts at the top of column 2. Although the head may then be lower on the page than is the start of the story, the eye will naturally go to the top of the second column as it moves from on one to the next.

★Keep the path from the end of the head to the start of the story as short and uncomplicated as possible.

Nowhere along that return sweep should the eye be distracted by art, editor's notes, blurbs or other magnets.

★ Use paragraph starters to direct the eye to the start of a story.

If there's any doubt whatsoever about directing of the eye to the start of the story, a "paragraph starter" may be used as a mild magnet to signal the proper starting point. Initials, gimcracks or spots of color are good devices.

The "blurb" is a magazine device that has been tried by some newspapers...though without conspicuous success. The blurb is set in display type but it is far longer than a headline. Usually it is in normal grammatical English sentences, not in headlinese. Many editors believe that a blurb is necessary to expand upon the terse headline, especially if it's a teaser or connotative one.

Placement of the blurb is a vexatious problem. Ideally it should be directly over the beginning of the article and, preferably, directly below the headline. Often this placement is not conducive to a pleasant page design.

Then the editor must rely on instinct to place it where it will contribute to the page pattern but not distract the eye away from the start of the body type.

★ Make sure that a dominant element holds the page together.

That "dominant element" may be the head itself or a picture. If there are two or more pictures on the page, the hen-and-chick principle previously discussed should be applied.

If there is only one picture, it is often most effective quite far removed from the headline. Art may be ganged into one area or widely dispersed. Such ganging is possible because normally there is only one story on a page or spread and so all the pictures will be related in subject matter.

★ Keep white space at the outside of the page or spread.

The irregular silhouette of the free page is its greatest charm. So all elements should be pushed into the center of the page, leaving its outline as ragged as possible.

★ Avoid trapped space.

"Trapped space" is a large area of white completely surrounded by typographic elements. Such a hole in the middle of a page gives the effect of an object disintegrating from centrifugal force and spinning off into space.

★ Fallow corners are effective as white areas.

Because the eye doesn't hasten to the top-right or lower-left corners in normal reading procedure, there is no great loss if these areas are left open. When they are blank, they accentuate the reading diagonal and that is pleasing to the eye.

★ Orient your layouts.

An "oriented layout" is familiarly called the "no-orphan technique" or the "buddy system". It means that every element in a layout aligns on a common axis with at least one other element. No element stands alone, as an "orphan".

The more axes held in common by the more elements, the more tightly the page is "woven".

Elements commonly align on their edges, be they type or pictures. When body type is aligned, it is on one or both margins as well as at the top or bottom of a leg of type. When display type is aligned, it is on the mass of the letter, rather than on an outside point. So a cap T would align on its stem, an M on its left leg and a B or R on its stem. But an A, V or W would align on an axis about halfway between the start of the left stroke and the vertex. An O aligns on an imaginary line about one-fifth of its diameter from the left.

If there is a prominent feature in a picture, orientation may be made at that point. The edge of a building, a prominent tree or post or a standing figure may be used for alignment. Lines of force may be harnessed and direct the eye right to another element; this is strong orientation.

★ Keep "empty sweeps" as short and simple as possible.

An "empty sweep" is the path of the eye from the end of one column of body type to the start of the next. Placement of a picture at the top or bottom of a leg can increase or diminish a sweep. It is less than ideal to make the eye jump over an entire column or columns that are occupied by art to get to continuation of body type. There ought to be a short tuck-in in every column to guide the eye across the page.

The main objective, of course, is to avoid confusing the reading eye. So, if the empty sweep is obvious and there are no distractions along that path, often these guidelines need not be followed rigidly.

★ Avoid widows at the head or foot of a leg of type.

For this purpose a widow is considered a line less than half filled. It is worth juggling elements to avoid positioning widows where they will create a jagged effect on the horizontal alignment.

Especially avoid an extremely short widow at the top of a leg where the empty sweep has been long. The reader feels cheated if he has to make a long sweep and finds just a fragment of a line—or even a word—up there.

★ Use white space to separate articles on a single spread.

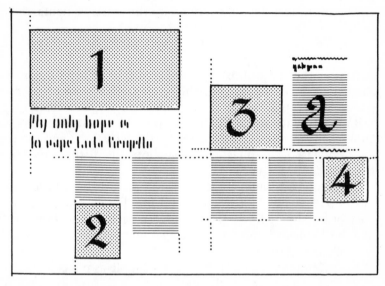

ORIENTED LAYOUT. Dotted lines show common axes shared by two or more elements. Head aligns with Photo 1. Column 2 of type aligns with photo at right margin and Column 1 aligns, at top, with Column 2 and vertically with Photo 2.

Photo 3 aligns on margin with Column 3 of type which in turn shares horizontal axis with Columns 1, 2 and 4 and Photo 4. Body type *a* may be sidebar to main story or separate piece; it aligns at bottom with Photo 3.

Note that each margin is defined: Photo 1 defines left side—as does head—and top. Photo 2 marks bottom and Photo 4, right margin.

THREE-ELEMENT SPREAD on single page displays each story prominently, with minimum competition from other stories and with maximum convenience for reader.

Often two or more articles must run on the same spread. They may be independent or the smaller ones may be "sidebars" to the main piece. These may be separated by running a rule—in black or in color—between them. Be sure that the rule has enough typographic color to brighten the page as well as separate items.

One of the items—usually a smaller one—can be boxed or run over a tint block, in color or gray.

★ A different typeface and a different column width will distinguish between two articles.

Sans Serifs is useful for such distinction, providing the mass is not so great it scares away the reader.

Unusually wide alleys or horizontal stripes may separate the articles. This is especially effective if they are run horizontally clear across the spread. The longer story usually runs at the top of the page.

★ Provide adequate margins on tint blocks.

A tint block, in color or gray, should be handled like a tiny page. It needs adequate margins. Just as we wouldn't run type to

SCALLOPED PAGES should have one leg of type defining lower margin. Dotted rectangles show how pictures may be part of type column or stand independently at bottom of page. Difference in lengths of adjacent columns must be obvious, minimum of 8 lines of type.

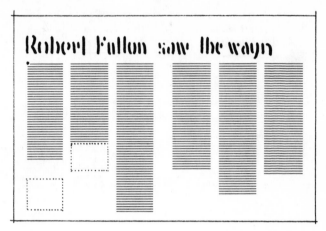

the very edge of a sheet of paper, so it shouldn't run to the edge of the tint block.

★ Place photos appropriate to the shooting angle.

If a photograph has been taken shooting sharply downward from a high vantage point, it will look inappropriate at the top of a page. Conversely, so will a shot made of a bird flying directly overhead should that picture run at the foot of the page.

★ Use scalloped pages.

A "scalloped page" is most useful when the editor has a lot of type and little, if any, art. To scallop a page, all columns in the spread are aligned at the top. But at the bottom they are deliberately not aligned. One column must touch the lower margin, all others are shorter. Adjacent columns must vary by at least 8 lines, otherwise the effect will be one of careless measurement rather than deliberate scalloping.

One-column pictures may be used at the foot of a column or at the lower margin. In the latter case, there should be at least 12 lines of type between the picture and the type in that column.

Decorative initials or other paragraph starters may be used in a scalloped page. The headline should extend past the halfway mark of the right-hand page.

★ Use gatefolds functionally.

The "gatefold" received its biggest boost when it was adopted by girlie magazines to give a larger area for the presentation of female nudity. It is created when six pages are printed on a single sheet and one third of the sheet is folded back to fit into the normal format. For typical magazines the gatefold is most economical when it's part of the cover.

For very small publications the gatefold may be the entire package. Then the editor has a series of layout problems. Page 1 is treated conventionally. As the reader then opens the book, pages 2 and 5 are revealed; they must be designed as a spread. As page 5, the back gatefold, is lifted, pages 3 and 4 come to view. These make a spread and they must tie in harmoniously with page 2. A danger of this format is that page 6 is an orphan and may be overlooked by the reader. Some editors avoid this by jumping an article to page 6 or using a reefer to direct the reader there.

★ The grid system is a useful crutch.

Using the "grid system", the editor divides the spread into rectangles. These start out as quarters or thirds vertically and horizontally of each page of the spread. Further subdividing may be done.

GATEFOLD on cover stock or within magazine. Inside, it is most effective and economical when it extends centerfold.

★ Don't break a page into equal areas.

The hen-and-chick principle applies here. One area subdivision of a spread should obviously be much larger than any other.

All heads align on a vertical and horizontal junction and body type and art occupy one or more rectangles. This applies the principle of oriented layouts and is a good way to get started on a layout when the wells of inspiration have temporarily gone dry.

★ Finger-trace the eye path.

After a layout has been made, the editor can check its effec-

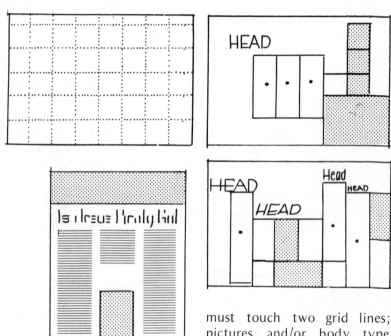

must touch two grid lines; pictures and/or body type blocks occupy complete rectangles. In diagram at right, rectangles marked with dots indicate body-type blocks. Subdividing pages into smaller grids allows greater flexibility in page patterns.

GRID SYSTEM for layouts divides spread into squares (here 40 full ones plus fractions at page-top). Headlines

tiveness by using a simple psychological procedure. Run your index finger down the column as the reader will consume the type. Deliberately lift the finger off the page for the empty sweep, as the eye goes to the start of the next leg of type. Then lower the finger onto the paper again. This simple exercise will emphasize those sweeps which are too long or where the path has been interrupted by some non-verbal element. It sounds Mickey Mousy but it works. And well!

A useful technique is to paste up a page of your magazine completely filled with body type alone. Make a same-size photostat of this—a "page matrix". Then, when you have a makeup problem, cut pieces of neutral gray construction paper to the exact size of available photographs after reduction.

By pushing these rectangles around on the matrix, by laying on headlines of appropriate size and form (clipped from a previous edition) and by creating open areas with pieces of white paper, it is easy to visualize the proposed page, not only in the mind's eye where it can be evaluated only by the editor but in a visual form that can be tried out on other people.

Bleed pictures are a common hallmark of magazine layout. Axioms for the use of pictures have been listed in Chapter 4. They are well worth following.

Magazines tend toward connotative heads but definitive ones are also useful. The same headline forms used by newspapers work well on free pages and slash heads are especially attractive.

Standing headings, like those used in a newspaper, should have a strong family resemblance.

Color is available more frequently for magazine use than in newspapers.

★ Use color functionally.

Color should be used to attract attention, to give emphasis, to guide the eye through all areas of a spread, to decorate the page and lure the reader into it.

★ Don't use color just because it's available.

★ Use color sparingly.

★ Use color in no more than three areas on a spread.

The area may be large but it should be simple and well defined.

★ Don't use color for body type.

And if color is used for headlines, be sure the hue is strong enough to carry the image well.

★ Avoid standard process colors for spot-color use.

"Process colors" are those used to reproduce all the hues of the spectrum as we see them in nature. Three "standard colors" are used, cyan, magenta and lemon. Black is added for detail and to strengthen shadow areas. Cyan and magenta, while strong enough to carry type, are irritating to the eye. So-called "off shades" of color are far more effective.

★ Use color for non-verbal elements.

Color is best when used for boxes, rules, tint blocks, ornaments, etc. Although the nameplate carries verbal matter, most people don't "read" the flag; they recognize it as an ideogram. So it does work well in color.

★ Avoid the Christmas syndrome.

Never, never, never print red type on green paper. Or on any other paper. Despite its too-wide Yuletime use, red type, especially on green paper, is cruel to the reading eye.

Expo art lends itself well to the use of color.

★ Don't print halftones in color.

Too much detail is lost. If halftones must be printed in color, make sure it is appropriate. A steak printed in blue looks most unappetizing; persons printed in that color look anemic. Orange icicles are ridiculous; so are green daisies.

★ Don't print black halftones over a tint block.

The result is a muddy color that is not at all pleasing.

★ Use duotones.

Duotones are made from a single black-and-white photo. Two plates are made; one is printed in black, the other in color. The result is a new, third color and the reproduction has sparkle and depth. Duotones are easy to prepare and to print and are kind to the budget.

Colored paper is available to most magazine editors but usually they will be wise to stick to white. When a color is chosen, it should be light enough to afford adequate visibility to black type and should be of a pure, clear hue.

Magazines may be printed on "newsprint", from which comes

124

TRAPPED SPACE is area just above lower picture. Such space tends to weaken layout by suggesting disintegration by centrifugal force.

the term "pulps" to describe commercial magazines of low quality and of supposedly lower standards of content. "Slick" magazines are printed on "coated" paper, one with a very smooth finish.

Coated papers are available in both shiny and dull or "matte" finish. Although it is popularly held that shiny paper is of the highest quality, it is less pleasant to read because reflected light may irritate the eyes.

Paper may be of differing "bulk". Paper is sold by the pound and the weight of paper is important, not only as it affects the production budget but as it changes postage costs, an ever-growing concern of editors.

Paper of the same weight may be relatively thin or thick. A bulkier paper may make a more impressive or pleasing package for the reader to hold without affecting postal costs. The "opacity" of paper must be dense enough to avoid "show-through", the shadow image of printing on the back of the sheet.

Many consumer magazines have a practice of printing a special section on paper distinctly different in color, texture and quality from that of the rest of the book. Non-commercial magazines have copied the usage. In many instances the results are less than optimal.

Uncoated paper of relatively poor quality is often used and such paper rarely offers true colors. The muddy hues we associate with this usage detract irritatingly from readability.

Even in quality papers, color may reduce visibility of type and even be irritating to the reading eye.

★ White paper and black ink are as close as feasible to the ideal combination.

This is especially true for newsprint.

So we come 'round the whole 360 degrees. Black-and-white is about as simple a combination as can be dreamed up. And that reiterates the KISS Axiom that has been the foundation for this whole book. Keep it simple!

The final criterion of journalistic excellence is always the simple question posed to the editor:

"Will the way I propose to do this make it more easy, convenient, pleasurable and rewarding for the reader?"

If the answer is "Yes!", the editor's job is well done and there is no necessity to evaluate it by other Axioms. But as guidelines to that ultimate goal of best serving the reader, the Axioms are valuable signposts.

Glossary

A

accent face, letterform of exaggerated weight or radically different form used to enliven headline schedule.

agate, 5½ point type. Also, any face used to set tabular matter in newspapers.

alley, strip of white space separating columns of type in newspaper or magazine page.

American Square Serifs, ethnic division of type race, in monotonal form with serifs heavier than regular strokes. *(See also Egyptian.)*

anchor, to place strong display elements in corners of pages.

appeals, small headlines on cover of magazine calling attention to articles inside.

armpit, to place narrow headline immediately under wider one. Also combination of headlines so created.

art, all pictorial matter in publication. Also, original copy for platemaker.

ascender, that portion of lowercase letter projecting above meanline. Also, letter itself that has such projection.

attention compellor, typographic element with strong visual attraction.

author's alteration, AA, any change in type not required to correct error of typesetter.

axis of orientation, A/O, vertical line at left of series of lines of type to which reading eye automatically returns to begin successive lines.

B

banner, large multicolumn head on front page, usually at least 4 columns wide.

baseline, that on which bottom of primary letters align.

basement, lower half of newspaper page, especially front or section.

Ben Day, system of adding dot or line pattern to line drawings by imprinting on negative or engraver's metal; named after inventor.

b.f., boldface.

bio note, small block of body type giving biographical and other information about author of article.

BL, body line, increment of measurement—height of one line of strikeon body type — for dummying pasteups.

Black Letter, race of type made of straight thick and thin lines meeting at sharp angles. Erroneously called Old English, which is one of its families.

bleed, picture which runs across margin and off page. Also, as verb, to place art in such position.

blurb, block of type larger than body, used to amplify or explain headline in magazine.

body, type of comparatively small size used in blocks of copy, as contrasted to display type of headlines.

boldface, letter of normal form and width but of heavier strokes.

border, plain or ornamental frame around advertising, etc. Border material is usually wider or more ornate than rules used for similar purpose.

bowl, circle or major part thereof in letterform, especially that which meets stem, as in *b* and *d*. Letters such as *a, e, g, and o* also have bowls.

box, typographic element surrounded on four sides, or top and bottom only, with border or rule.

breaker head, divider, large subhead usually at least 14-point.

bright, short, interesting, often humorous editorial feature.

bucket head, one placed in opening created when first and last columns of body type run alongside of, and as high as, headline.

buddy system, oriented layout (*which see*).

budget, all news and feature articles and art available for current issue of publication.

bulk, to make publication seem larger by using paper of same weight but greater thickness per sheet.

bullet, large period used as typo-graphic ornament.

bump, to tombstone or armpit heads (*which see*).

C

Canadian wrap, system of sub-dividing longer story into series of 2-leg units under 2-column subhead.

canopy, to run headline across picture and horizontally adjacent story.

captions, explanatory matter accompanying pictures. Most commonly used for magazines; in newspapers usually called cutlines.

catchline, line of display type between picture and cutlines.

center spread, two facing pages at center of section of newspaper or magazine.

chimney, series of heads and/or pictures of same width stacked to fill entire page depth.

chopped head, one of two or more lines of varying column width.

column rule, thin vertical division line between columns on newspaper page.

combination, combo, two or more related pictures grouped as single element.

common diagonal, system of scaling pictures that uses principle that all rectangles of same proportions have diagonal at the same angle to horizon.

constants, those typographic elements which are same in all issues of newspaper, i.e., nameplate, masthead, folio lines, etc.

continuous tone, picture made of modulated shades of gray or color, such as photograph, and contrasting to line art such as pen-and-ink sketch.

copy factor, numerical designation of ratio to determine length of type column produced by given amount of typewritten copy.

copy log, record of all copy sent to typesetter and platemaker.

crop, to eliminate unwanted areas in photograph by actually cutting or, most frequently, by indicating them with marginal marks.

cutlines, explanatory matter accompanying pictures. In magazines usually called captions.

cutoff rule, thin, horizontal dividing lines in page. Also, printing element that places such image on paper. Often "rule" is omitted.

cyan, vivid blue used for filtering and printing process color.

D

descender, portion of lowercase letter projecting below baseline. Also, letter which has such projection.

dogleg, column projecting from rectangular area of body type.

dominant head, heaviest one on inside page, which acts as nucleus for page pattern.

dummy, drawn guide that printer follows to produce page pattern designed by editor. Also, to draw such guide.

duotone, color-printing technique which creates single image from two impressions, one in dark ink, usually black, other in light hue. Both plates are made from single black-and-white photograph, unlike 2-color process plates.

Dutch wrap, continuation of body type to column at right not covered by headline.

E

em, blank space in square of size of type. Called mutton or mut to avoid confusion with en. Erroneously, synonym for pica.

empty sweep, path of eye as it moves, with nothing to read, from one column or area of page to another.

en, vertical half of em. Called nut to avoid confusion with em.

expo art (for expository), charts, graphs, diagrams, etc.

F

face, style of type.

fallow corner, top right and lower left of page.

flag, nameplate, name of newspaper in display form on page one. Erroneously called masthead (*which see*).

flatout, 1-up technique (*which see*).

folio lines, technically page numbers but in common usage includes volume and number, date, and name of publication in small type on inside pages.

font, collection of type characters required to set copy in one size and face.

formal page, one arranged so typographic elements fill entire rectangular area within margins.

format, general appearance of publication, especially page size and number of columns.

free page, one in which type and pictures are not arranged in conventional columns.

G

gatefold, page of magazine larger than regular ones, folded one or more times so it does not project beyond the edges.

grid, layout system dividing area into rectangles, then starting each typographic element at corner of one area.

gutter, margins between facing pages.

H

hairline, thinnest rule used in publications, thinnest stroke in letterform.

halftone, technique for reproducing continuous-tone originals by pattern of dots or lines of various sizes and proximity. Also, any picture so reproduced.

hammer, reverse kicker, short one-line head, twice as large as the main head which is below and to right.

head, abbreviation for headline. Also, margin at top of page.

heading, label or standing heads, often ornamented.

headletter, typeface used for headlines.

headline, display type that seeks to attract the reader into body type usually by summarizing story.

headline schedule, hed sked, all headline forms used by a publication, usually grouped by column-widths.

hen-and-chicks, layout principle in which definitely larger picture is nucleus of pattern of smaller ones around it.

hood, 3-sided box around headline.

HTK, head to come.

hue, that characteristic which identifies colors to human eye.

I

i&e, identification-and-exposition lines (*which see*).

identification-and-exposition lines, ident-and-expo, picture identification in which first (ident) line gives name of subject and second (expo) gives terse explanation of news interest.

indicia, legal data indicating publications qualifications for second-class mailing privileges and other information about rates, frequency, etc.

initial, first letter in word set in larger and more decorative face. *(See inset and rising initial.)*

inset initial, sunken initial, large letter occupying area cut out of top left corner of mass of body type.

inside spread, center spread (*which see*).

Italic, form of Roman type race which slants to right. Used erroneously to indicate all slanted type, which in other races correctly is Oblique.

J

jam, to place headlines so they touch each other. *(See tombstone and armpit.)*

jump, to continue story from one page, usually the front, to another. Also, story so continued.

jumpover, placement of picture or other element within column of body type that requires eye to move across such interruption to continue reading.

jump head, headline on continued portion of a story.

jump line, line in body type that indicates story has been continued from earlier page.

jump the gutter, layout technique to tie facing pages into single oriented composition.

justify, to set type so left and right margins are straight. Also, to make all columns in page same length.

K

kicker, small head, usually underscored, above and slightly to left of main head.

L

layout, pattern of elements in printing form. Also, written

diagram instructs printer how to produce such form. Also, as two words, act of producing such patterns.

lc, lowercase (*which see*).

lca, lowercase-alphabet length, length in points of line of type including all minuscules of font.

leader (leeder), row of dots or dashes connecting two or more elements in tabulations, such as name of stock and its price.

ledd (phonetic spelling for lead, piece of metal that creates 6 points of blank space), to add interlineal spacing to affect readability or to justify column.

leed (phonetic spelling for lead), first part of news story which usually gives all major information in summary form. Also, main story or editorial in issue or on page.

leg, vertical subdivision of mass of body type arranged in several columns. Also, lower diagonal strokes of *R* and *K*.

legibility, that quality which makes it easy for reader to see and comprehend comparatively few printed characters as in headline.

letterspacing, additional spacing between letters in word.

library, all typefaces available to editor in printing or typesetting plant.

linear definition, line cut made from continuous-tone art.

line cut, photoengraving in simple masses of black and white, as opposed to halftone (*which see*).

lines of force, arrangements of elements within picture that tend to direct eye in certain directions.

logo, abbreviation of logotype. Also, publication's nameplate. Also, identification of page or section, i.e., women's or sports.

M

magazine, layout style in which elements are often not in regular column increments and in which large areas of white space are used for display effect.

magenta, red hue used for filtering and printing process color.

masthead, collection of information including name of publisher of newspaper, time and place of publication, etc. Erroneously used to refer to nameplate.

measure, length of line of type.

mechanical, pasteup dummy (*which see*).

minuscule, small letters of alphabet.

mortice, to cut area out of halftone plate so that type or another picture may be inserted. Such opening cut out of the corner of rectangular plate is notch or external mortice. Opening completely surrounded by plate is internal mortice; that surrounded on three sides is bay.

N

naked column, one without a headline or art at its top.

nameplate, flag, logo, name of publication in display form as it appears on page one or cover. Erroneously called masthead.

no-orphan technique, oriented layout (*which see*).

notch, mortise that removes rectangle from one corner of halftone plate.

O

1-up, layout technique which uses one more column of space than of type; also called flatout.

opacity, degree to which sheet of paper allows show-through of printing on reverse side.

optical center, point 10% above mathematical center of page.

optical magnets, typographic elements of strong interest to readers.

optimum format, one which uses body type in measure at or near optimum line length.

optimum line length, that which is easiest to read, at higher speed, with lower fatigue and with maximum comprehension.

oriented layout, buddy system, no-orphan technique, one in which all elements are studiedly aligned on common vertical and horizontal axes.

Oxford rule, border consisting of heavy and light rule in parallel pairs.

P

paragraph starter, decorative initial or other device that leads eye to start of unindented paragraph.

pasteon, disposable cold-type characters arranged and affixed to a mechanical.

pasteup, mechanical, detailed dummy made by affixing same-size element onto paper as instructions to, or actual photographic copy for, platemaker.

point, unit of printer's measurement, approximately 1/72 inch, actually .01384.

pica, 12 points.

porkchop, thumbnail, half-column portrait.

precede, also preseed, explanatory matter that runs before news story.

prepack, technique of making up editorial matter as advertising is, free from normal column increments, and well in advance of use.

preseed, precede (*which see*).

primary letter, minuscules without ascenders or descenders.

primary optical area, POA, top left corner of page or subdivision thereof, where reading eye first enters.

process color, system of printing three primary colors to reproduce full spectrum of nature.

progression, general arrangement of contents in publication.

proof, rough print of type or plate used to detect errors. Also, relatively hastily made photoprint to show content of negative.

pyramid, advertising on newspaper page. Also, pattern for arranging advertising roughly as one or two triangles on page. Also, abbreviation for inverted pyramid, headline form.

R

readability, characteristic which makes it easy to read large masses of body type.

read-in, style of cutlines in which display type is part of sentence continued in body size.

reefer, line or two of type, set into news story, that refers reader to associated material elsewhere in paper.

reverse, printing plate or area with black or colored background on which type appears in white. Also, photographic or chemical process that converts black-on-white image to white-on-black.

reverse kicker, hammer (*which see*).

ribbon, shallow horizontal area, especially that no deeper than 2 inches, above newspaper ad not quite full page deep.

rising initial, stickup initial, first letter of word in large size and/or ornamental form that aligns with first line of body type and projects above type block.

rough, rough dummy, sketchy same-size drawing showing placement of typographic elements in form.

roundup, collection of small items on similar topic combined into single story or running under single headline.

rule, element that prints line or lines simpler than those of border.

runaround, body type set at various measures so it forms opening into which picture or display type can be inserted.

run-in, technique in which catchline becomes part of sentence continuing in cutlines.

S

sandwich, interpolated notice in column of body type calling reader's attention to associated material on other pages. Usually enclosed with decorative rules top and bottom.

scallop, page pattern in which all columns align at top but vary markedly in depth.

schedule, headline, hed sked, all headlines used in newspaper.

screen, device used to reduce continuous-tone original art to halftone plate. Also, designation for fineness of halftone so produced, e.g., 85-line screen indicates plate with 85 rows of halftone dots per linear inch. Also, to reduce tone of black areas of art or type by superimposing pattern of white dots on printing surface.

self cover, magazine or booklet on which cover is of same paper as all other pages.

serif, small finishing stroke at end of main strokes of letter.

spread, double spread, two facing pages, especially in magazine or book. Center spread is one at center of publication so both pages are printed on same sheet.

S/S, same size, instruction to platemaker.

stickup initial, rising initial (*which see*).

stock, paper used for printing job. Stock cover of magazine or booklet is one on paper heavier than that of inside pages.

straight matter, body composition as contrasted to display matter. Also, editorial matter as contrasted to advertising.

sunken initial, inset initial (*which see*).

surprint, matter printed, usually in black, upon background of color or halftone.

T

tabloid, tab, newspaper format with page approximately 11 x 15 inches. Also, journalistic approach concentrating on frothy content and flashy display.

terminal area, TA, lower right portion of printed page.

30-dash, typographic device indicating end of story in typewritten or typeset form.

time matter (short for anytime), that feature copy which does not demand immediate use.

tint block, printing element that lays down simple mass of color, with no detail, over which is surprinted type or art.

tombstone, bumped headlines side by side.

tone, value, relative darkness of page or block of type or photograph.

tower, chimney, vertical arrangement of horizontal elements in newspaper page.

trapped space, area of white space completely surrounded by typographic elements.

tripod, headline form of a single line of large type at immediate left of two lines of smaller type.

turn over, continuation of magazine article from one page to its reverse side.

tuck-in, placement of picture to right of headline so story wraps from under head to under art.

typeface, reference to type stressing style or design.

type library, all type faces and rules, borders, and ornaments available for use in one printing establishment or for one publication.

typo, abbreviation of typographic error.

typographic error, error in setting made by typesetter.

typography, basic philosophy regarding use of printing elements.

U

u&lc, upper-and-lowercase, style of setting type which capitalizes each word.

underscored, typographic elements, especially headlines, which are given added weight by a rule immediately beneath them.

W

wicket, headline with two short lines of small type immediately at left of single larger line.

widow, type line shorter than full measure, usually 50% or less.

woven page, one in which no alley extends full depth of page.

wraparound, magazine cover design which continues from front cover to back.